Tell Me Another Tale

Further Reflections on the Church of God

By Merle D. Strege

Warner Press, Inc.
Anderson, Indiana

Copyright © 1993 by Warner Press, Inc.
ISBN #0-87162-649-7   Stock #D 4202
All rights reserved
Printed in the United States of America
Warner Press, Inc.

Arlo F. Newell, Editor in Chief
Dan Harman, Book Editor
Cover by Larry Lawson
Interior Art by Dave Liverett

Previous Book in this series:

Tell Me the Tale, Historical Reflections on the Church of God,
D4200, by Merle D. Strege, published by Warner Press, Inc.1991.

Dedicated to

Thomas N. Pappas
and
Frederick v. Shoot

Table of Contents

Introduction

This volume is the second collection of my essays which Warner Press has graciously consented to publish. An initial invitation to speak or write always elicits feelings of warmth and appreciation, but the demonstrated willingness to publish a sequel is particularly gratifying. I am very mindful of the fact that my work benefits richly from the interest, support, and encouragement of a host of people. At the top of this list is the Editorial division of Warner Press, and I must begin by acknowledging my debt to that fine and interesting group.

My academic and personal lives converge at the point of friendship. I am privileged to have friends who have incarnated many of the ideas which I attempt to teach men and women in my classes at Anderson University. Many of those students have heard some of the themes presented here with sufficient repetition as to prompt them to beg for relief, but their questions and comments have helped me refine my ideas, and for those criticisms I am grateful. Other students, particularly those in my courses in the history of the Church of God, have presented research papers that have stimulated my own research. Some of those topics also have found their way into this book, and I want to acknowledge here the debt that a graduate school professor incurs to interested and inquisitive students. The academic friendship of students and professors is one of the chief joys of teaching.

I also am indebted to many friends, most of whom are serving the Church of God movement in academic capacities. Many of these people listen to my ideas with a critical ear and offer suggestions for their improvement. All of them, whether they live in Anderson or some other place, have offered me the support that colleagues give one another, and it is my deep privilege to name them as such: the faculty of the Department of Bible, Religion and Philosophy (my new academic home) at Anderson University and the faculty of the School of Theology at Anderson. I must also name specifically Cole Dawson, Arthur Kelly, Willard Reed, Russ Skaggs, Spencer Spaulding, Doug Welch, and Richard Willowby. Each in his own way cares deeply about the church, and if it is true that something of people's character may be known by their friends then I am proud to be known by my friendships with these men and their commitments.

The debts of people who write take many forms. Two have already been named and several more still remain. I am deeply conscious of the influence of others on my own ideas. Footnotes and endnotes customarily document this kind of indebtedness. I hope that my essays will prompt some of those who read them to further reading and reflection. I can think of no better way to repay some of the debt I owe to the people who live in the citations of this small collection than that I refer interested readers to the works cited herein. They contain many more ideas which are more extensively pursued than readers will likely encounter here.

I owe another kind of debt to the people who have invited me to speak at ministers' meetings, conferences, and camp meetings. Some people seem to write out of an overflow of ideas; they appear to be incapable of *not* writing. I am neither so creative or blessed. Without assignments I would write very little. Thus invitations to speak or write help me a great deal in that they prompt me to get on with my work. Each of the essays published here was originally written for another audience. The bulk of these first appeared as my regular column in *Vital Christianity*. Chapter 1 was originally prepared for the Open Forum of the Independent Christian Churches/Churches of Christ in Indianapolis in March 1989. It was read in a slightly amended version for the Central States Ministers' Meeting in St. Joseph, Michigan, in March of 1993. Chapter 6 first saw the light of day as a presentation at the Church of God Associate Ministers' National Retreat in 1990. Chapter 7 is a reworked version of a set of lectures first prepared for the Warner Press Curriculum Writers' Conference in 1992. In the case of each presentation, people who heard it graciously encouraged me to edit these papers for publication, and I have taken their encouragement at face value. The invitations originally extended to me gave me the occasions to think about these matters, and to those who extended them I am also indebted.

I hope that it will not be lost on those who take time to read this introduction that the church, or some one of its constituent groups, has provided the immediate context and occasion for much of what

I write. Thus it is no accident that the Church of God specifically, but also the wider church in the United States, provides the theme that organizes this collection of essays. It is surely a cliché, but nonetheless true, to say that we live in troubling times. Perhaps people always are troubled by the times of their lives. The enormous pressures which our society rests on the church trouble me. Some of what I have written reflects that sense of trouble. But I also have written out of the deep conviction that the church stands over against the world as the earnest and witness of the kingdom of God. The church, as that witness, is the last and best hope of the world. In other words I write about the church, at times critically, to encourage, not complain.

My first collection of essays, *Tell Me the Tale*, was organized around matters concerning theological ethics. Accordingly, the virtues of the people of God played a prominent role in that work. In this sequel, which attends more to the corporate and institutional life of the church, the focus shifts from virtues to practices. The church's practices have to do with its social and public life. They are collective activities in pursuit of the ends for which the church exists. Many such practices order the life of the church. Some of them have been described forcefully and with great insight by James McClendon (1986) and L. Gregory Jones (1990). To their ideas I wish to add, with more than a little temerity, four additional practices: witness, politics, familial relationships, and "timefulness." These are treated in chapters two through five.

I make no claim to be a systematic theologian. First and foremost I am an ordinary, garden-variety, narrative historian whose primary field of endeavor is the Church of God (Anderson). A narrative church historian will, it seems to me, inevitably converge historical interests with ideas both theological and ethical. This convergence also explains why I have not attempted to write with the systematician's analytical concerns. Rather, I have tried to approach the second part of this collection as a historical theologian. I am encouraged in this attempt by the conviction that the church is a story-formed community. This is doubly true of the Church of God movement, my spiritual home and through whose narratives and traditions I have learned to interpret the larger Christian tradition, all the way back to the Bible. To mention this nurture is to acknowledge still another debt.

Other people also contribute much to my life in ways that make possible my academic and church work. Mrs. Joyce Krepshaw, Faculty Secretary at the School of Theology at Anderson University, typed many drafts of several of the essays printed here. That she willingly took even the latest of changes in manuscripts is testimony to the grace she brings to the seminary. My wife, Fran, found many of the photographs reproduced in this volume, allowing me time to work on the text itself. She is far more than a research assistant, capable as she is at those tasks. Along with our two fine sons, Ike and Pete, Fran helps me perceive how self-centered and pre-occupied with my own interests I really am. Their tolerance of my many shortcomings also teaches me about the limitless possibilities for practicing the Christian virtues. These three people who share a roof with me have often displayed for my sake the virtue of longsuffering. As any student of the Bible knows, that is a virtue of the strong, not the powerless.

During the academic year 1992-93, Anderson University celebrated its seventy-fifth anniversary. As an alumnus, I look back fondly on my student days at what we then called "AC." The intellectual ferment of those days produced new discoveries, new friendships, new interests, and a new yearning for an academic career. The men to whom this book is dedicated each took seriously my halting undergraduate efforts at scholarship. Each extended to me his academic friendship. Each gave me opportunities for some early ventures in teaching. Each encouraged my pursuit of further study. On the occasion of Anderson University's Diamond Jubilee I am pleased to acknowledge, with gratitude and affection, the debts a student owes to those he has been privileged to call mentor.

Merle D. Strege
Camp Meeting 1993

I

Practices of the People of God

Some Reflections on the Church of God (Anderson)

The Church of God (Anderson, Ind.)[1] can point to certain paradigmatic events as statements of its central convictions. Two of these involve the ministry of Daniel S. Warner (1842-1895). While Church of God people think it inappropriate to refer to him or anyone else as the movement's founder, they nevertheless name Warner more frequently than any other of the early pioneers. Our institutions, whether publishing house or colleges, memorialize him more frequently than any other person. Warner held membership in the Indiana State Holiness Association, one of the numerous affiliates of that loose fellowship originally known as the National Camp Meeting Association for the Promotion of Christian Holiness. But Warner attended the May 20-21, 1881, meeting of the association armed with an amendment to its constitution. His motion would have removed from the articles of membership the stipulation that association members must have good standing in a religious denomination. This "sect-endorsing clause" constituted an implicit endorsement of the whole denominational structure of American Protestantism. As such, in Warner's mind, it contradicted the very spirit of perfect love, the presence of which in their hearts was the very claim of the sanctified members of the association. This contradiction proved too

7

severe for Warner to bear. When the Holiness Association voted down his resolution, he felt he had no option but to resign his membership.

Despite Warner's formal severance from the holiness movement, one must recognize the deep indebtedness of one side of his thought to the resurgent Wesleyanism of post-Civil War America. Even before the war, the holiness movement had reclaimed one side of John Wesley's teaching on the subject of entire sanctification.[2] Methodists such as Adam Clarke, he of commentary fame, emphasized Wesley's idea that the believer's entire sanctification, or "perfect love," could be realized in an instantaneous infusion of the empowering grace of God subsequent to the experience of justification and regeneration. It was this idea that gave rise to the characteristic holiness movement phrases "second blessing" and "second work of grace."

Warner's debt to the holiness movement's understanding of the doctrine of entire sanctification is readily apparent (Cf. *Bible Proofs* n.d.). Like other holiness preachers he understood salvation to encompass both justification and entire sanctification. Thus to be saved meant deliverance from both sin's condemnation and its power (n.d., *Salvation* 17-26). As Warner put the matter, " 'a good tree cannot bring forth evil fruit, nor an evil tree good fruit.' Therefore he whose life brings forth sin, is a sinner and not a Christian."[3]

The holiness movement's theology of sanctification was susceptible to challenge by Methodists as a less than accurate reading of Wesley, but for an ordained minister of the General Eldership of Churches of God such a theology invited charges of heresy. Warner had experienced conversion during a protracted meeting—a revival—held by an evangelist of the General Eldership near Montpelier, Ohio, in 1865. Within a year and a half he felt called to the ministry. Subsequently he received his ministerial license in October of 1867. The General Eldership had come into being in 1825 through the labor of John Winebrenner.[4] A German Reformed pastor, Winebrenner zealously practiced the new measures of revivalism spreading throughout American Protestantism during the Second Great Awakening. But his revivalist practices eventually led to his withdrawal from the German Reformed Church and the formation of a denomination of free standing congregations which he desired to be known simply by the biblical name "Church of God." "For Winebrenner then, the underlying or motivating principle in the establishment of these independent churches soon came to be thought of as the restoration of primitive or Biblical Christianity" (Kern:1974, 45).

The doctrine of the church taught by the Churches of God provided the other major source of D. S. Warner's theology. Winebrenner thought that "divisions among christians (*sic*), or a plurality of sects, are contrary to the doctrine of Christ, which teaches unity and oneness of His people."[5] "Primitive [New Testament] Christians" were joined in one united church, and their example Winebrenner understood as normative for latter day followers of Christ. In the pamphlet *The Church of God* Warner restated several Winebrennarian themes but recast them in the light of his Wesleyan experience of entire sanctification. Thus Warner argued that the love shed abroad in the hearts of believers by the Holy Spirit is the "bond of perfectness," which restores the unity of the church (n.d., *The Church of God* 21).

Warner's experience of sanctification prompted his revision of the Churches of God doctrine of the church. But because the Churches of God did not hold a doctrine of entire sanctification, Warner found himself charged with heterodoxy. In 1878, the West Ohio Eldership of the Churches of God revoked his license. Later that year Warner took fellowship with the Northern Indiana Eldership of the Churches of God. This group had broken with the General Eldership over the question whether Christians could join secret societies. The Northern Indiana Eldership also was congenial toward the doctrine of entire sanctification. Warner quickly rose to prominence in the small group and became joint editor and publisher of the Eldership's paper, *The Herald of Gospel Freedom*. The *Herald* merged with another paper, *The Pilgrim*, to form *The Gospel Trumpet* the first issue of which appeared in January, 1881, with Warner as editor.

Later in 1881 a second paradigmatic event occurred in the history of the Church of God. In October, at a Northern Indiana Eldership meeting near Beaver Dam in northern Indiana, Warner declared himself free of all forms of humanly devised church organization. He resolved to be a member of the Church of God "according to the New Testament plan." Five other persons accepted his invitation to join him. That same month, at Carson City, Michigan, Joseph and Allie Fisher along with their friend D. S. Warner, led a group out of a congregation of the Northern Michigan Eldership. In these two separate but related meetings the movement that has come to be known as the Church of God (Anderson, Ind.) had been born. That birth was the child of a marriage of two different theological traditions. To an essentially Wesleyan soteriology Warner had joined a restorationist ecclesiology that closely resembled that of the believers' churches.

One other word must be said about formative sources of the Church of God. Warner's marriage of Wesleyan soteriology and free church ecclesiology was nurtured in an ethos of revivalism. The Church of God came into being just as the revival began to shift from a routine expression of American religious fervor and church life to the carefully planned product of the efforts of teams of paid professionals. Charles Finney had died in 1876, only to be succeeded in national stature by D. L. Moody. The influence of revivalism on American Protestantism, and especially a new religious movement like the Church of God, should not be underestimated. Moreover, the holiness movement had adopted the camp meeting, the institution of frontier revivalism, as its primary vehicle of extension and organization. Holiness preachers conceived the closest possible association between the doctrine of holiness and the camp meeting. Thus they frequently attributed the decline in Methodism's emphasis on holiness to a parallel decline in the number and fervency of Methodist camp meetings. All this is to say that the ethos of the Church of God is what might be termed camp meeting revivalism. This ethos markedly shapes the movement's conception of what constitutes valid worship and good preaching, to name but two elements of church life.

A Reason for Being

To consider the Church of God movement's sense of its reason for being is to be aware of the presence of a powerful mythos at work in the Church of God. We have said that the reason for our being was to call divided Christians out of denominations into the one New Testament church. According to this mythos we have been far more perceptive of division than we have of witnesses to the church's oneness. For example, we commonly refer to the dark days of competitive denominationalism in late nineteenth century America. Now it surely is the case that denominational rivalries then were very strong. But in our focus on division we have failed to see movements of unity that also existed in the last quarter of the nineteenth century. Were there no restorationist churches witnessing to the unity of the New Testament church in 1881? Of course there were, but Warner saw them as likely candidates for the role of opponent in a debate. The holiness movement also transcended denominational barriers, as did Evangelicalism in general and the Evangelical Alliance in particular. However, Warner seems to have ignored these hopeful signs of Christian unity that were contemporary with him in favor of a darker view of a hopelessly divided Christendom. The Church of God has tended strongly to follow uncritically Warner's reading of the situation as that which called it forth.

The fourth editor of the *Gospel Trumpet*, Charles E. Brown (1883-1971), offered a different interpretation of the reason for the Church of God's existence. Succinctly put, D. S. Warner hated organization (1951: 101). A more positive way of stating the same point is that Warner had "discovered one great spiritual principle, which was the identification of the visible and invisible church in a spiritual congregation of Christians from which no Christian was excluded by any man-made rules or corporate forms of organization."[6] There is no question that early Church of God people harbored a deep suspicion of all forms of ecclesiastical organization. Congregational meetings that elected church officers were strictly forbidden; even the method of choosing leaders by ballot was condemned. Instead they believed and taught that God organized the church through the charismatic gifting of individuals, as St. Paul taught in 1 Corinthians 12. Through the exercise of their specific gifts, they believed, women and men identified their places of service in the body of Christ. No other organization was required, nor did any "human" organization exist other than the incorporated Gospel Trumpet Company during the first twenty-five years of the existence of the Church of God movement.

In terms of the Church of God's self-understanding, two differ-ent interpretations of the movement's reason for being can be locat-ed within the thought of the first generation, both of them influ-enced by Warner. Two of the movement's gospel songs may be taken as representative of these points of view. The first of these is presented in Warner's early song, "The Bond of Perfectness." Based on Colossians 3:14, this song celebrates the love planted in the human heart by the Holy Spirit, the Sanctifier. "No power of earth or hell, withal, can rend us from each other" or destroy per-fect love, "the bond of heaven's union." Thus we may sing:

> Beloved, how this perfect love
> Unites us all in Jesus!
> One heart, and soul, and mind: we prove
> The union heaven gave us.
> —*Worship the Lord*, no. 330

The Church of God's reason for being, we may conclude from this song, is to witness to the presence of the sanctifying Spirit as the agent of Christian unity. Our witness to the presence of the Spirit's love becomes the instrument by which the lost unity of the New Testament church will be restored. This profoundly simple insight gave the Church of God its early mission.

Another gospel song, William G. Schell's "Biblical Trace of the Church"[7] (1911:498), illustrates a second *raison d'etre* which took hold of the movement. This song rests upon a specialized exegesis of the apocalyptic books of both Old and New Testaments. About 1885 or 1886, when the Gospel Trumpet Company resided first in Williamston and especially later in Grand Junction, Michigan, members of the Gospel Trumpet "family" began encountering Adventist preachers and literature. As the number and intensity of these contacts increased, Church of God writers, and Warner in particular, became familiar with Adventist theological positions. One that especially intrigued him was the interpretation of Daniel and the Revelation offered in the work of Uriah Smith. The method Smith used would now be classified as a species of church-histori-cal exegesis. According to this method, biblical apocalyptic is regarded as a map of the history, both past and future, of the church. This is not the world-historical method of dispensationalism, but an interpretation focused particularly on the church and its history. Smith used this method to unlock the prophetic secrets of Daniel and the Revelation. The result of his work validated the existence of Adventism as foretold by the Bible itself.

Warner read Smith's book (1882) and made use of its typology in a manuscript he began but did not live to complete. H. M. Riggle (1872-1952), one of the leading preachers and controversialists in the Church of God movement, finished Warner's project and published it under the title *The Cleansing of the Sanctuary* (1903). Warner employed his own interpretation of the exegetical system he had learned from Uriah Smith and developed a prophetic rationale for the existence of the Church of God. The lines of this schematization of history appear in Schell's gospel song. In broad outline, that schematization runs as follows: The Christian church enjoyed a golden age of gospel purity until A.D. 270 when it fell into apostasy. The papal monarchy of the Roman Catholic church was the very essence of this corruption, and it held the true church in darkness for 1,260 years. In the year 1530 Lutheranism formalized itself according to the Augsburg Confession, and the power of the papacy was broken. Still, Protestantism represented but a partial restoration of the true church's purity. Not until the evening light of the Church of God reformation in 1880, 350 years after the Augsburg Confession, was the New Testament church fully restored.[8]

By applying the church-historical method in this fashion, Warner and others were able to provide the Church of God with a powerful *raison d'etre*. Their interpretation allowed the Church of God to understand itself as the product of a powerful outpouring of the Spirit of God in the last days before the return of the Lord. The Spirit was at work gathering all the saints of God into one holy family before the final judgment. Out of this self-understanding, many in the Church of God movement regarded it as the sign and instrument of this divine activity, as the Scriptures themselves foretold. Possessed of such a self-understanding, Church of God preachers boldly applied the biblical injunction, "Come out from among them, and be ye separate, saith the Lord" (2 Cor. 6:17) to those still living in denominational division. There could be no sin in the church; division sinned against the body of Christ; the only remedy for this condition was salvation understood as the "double cure" of justification and sanctification. Salvation alone was the door into the church, the bride of Christ, without spot or wrinkle.

So it came to be that two major viewpoints, related but distinct, offered the Church of God movement a reason for being. The earlier of these self-understandings simply merged the idea of holiness with a call to restore the lost unity of the New Testament church. In this view, the purpose of the Church of God (Anderson, Ind.) is to preach biblical holiness as the means of divided Christendom's return to wholeness. The prominence of the theme of love should not be interpreted to signify soft preaching or an inclusive view of the church. Worldliness was condemned in no uncertain terms and the church was proclaimed to be exclusive of all sin. Closely related, but distinct from this initial self-understanding was the more apocalyptic rationale that developed later. Holiness and unity retained their primary importance in this rationale, but they tended to be overshadowed by an exegetical method that located the movement's self-understanding in apocalyptic literature and the unfolding of history rather than in a *telos* or mission. This latter viewpoint became widely accepted in the Church of God through the work of the third editor of the *The Gospel Trumpet*, F. G. Smith (1880-1947). His book *The Revelation Explained* (1908) became the major expression of the church-historical self-understanding of the Church of God. It is not too much to say that this understanding was normative in the decade 1920 to 1930, the last year of which was also Smith's last as editor.

Attitudes Toward Other Church Bodies

The two self-understandings of the Church of God movement have worked themselves out in two very different attitudes toward other Christian bodies. In the movement's early decades both the "love works unity" theme and the church-historical theme benefited from the strongly held conviction that all who were truly saved should come out of "sect-Babylon," a term used to denote the entire structure of denominational Christianity. To continue one's membership in a denomination was every bit as much a sin against God as theft or adultery.[9] Since that was the case, it was incumbent on any saved person to flee Babylon and to refrain from "coming out" placed one's salvation in jeopardy.[10]

The logic of "come-outism" entailed the rejection of all other Christian churches as sects. Any sect was only a section of the body of Christ and therefore by definition not the whole. Warner believed strongly that humanly devised doctrines and systems of organization were the villains in this tragedy. But regardless of their causes, "since God's word renounces sects, they cannot be his church" (*The Church of God*: 27). By this argument the Church of God's theology of the church constituted a negative judgment on virtually all other church groups. About the best that could be said of them was that they lived up to the light they had. But the movement judged such groups to be largely in the dark.

The church-historical self-understanding reinforced Warner's exclusivist conception of the church to a point where, after 1920, some ministers began worrying that the Church of God movement was developing the same sectarian spirit on a creedal foundation that it had earlier condemned. One of the earliest expressions of this uneasiness came from the pen of George P. Tasker (1872-1958), missionary to India and one of the Church of God's brightest intellectual lights. Tasker did not share the majority opinion in the movement in favor of the church-historical self-understanding. He stated his views in sermons delivered in the United States while he and his wife, Minnie, were on furlough. After the Taskers' return to India a vigorous correspondence developed between Mr. Tasker and the *Gospel Trumpet* editorial office. Finally, in a pamphlet of 1924 Tasker published an opinion shared but not yet voiced by others:

> I tell you only the sober truth when I say that the people of the most sectarian mind and attitude that I have ever met in all my life have been and are just those people who have most fully imbibed our doctrine and spirit of geographical come-outism. . . . We have called for separations too often, not because the Holy Ghost was really leading that way at the time, but simply because of our doctrinal position on the point (1924:1).

Over the course of the ensuing five years more ministers began stating their reservations about the attitude toward other churches implicit in come-outism. Finally, E. A. Reardon (1874-1946), pastor of a congregation in Denver, delivered a sermon at Anderson Camp Meeting in 1929, wherein he expressed his belief that were Christ once again on earth he would not confine his activity to the Church of God movement.[11] That the General Ministerial Assembly afterwards voted Reardon off virtually every board on which he sat amply demonstrates the presence and strength of the opposite view. Nevertheless, the number of people who shared the reservations of Tasker, Reardon, and others was growing.

The Publication Board of the Church of God did not re-elect F. G. Smith to another term as editor in 1930. The man eventually chosen to succeed him, Charles E. Brown, sympathized with the views of Tasker and Reardon. During his more than two decades in the editor's chair, Brown challenged the church-historical self-understanding and "come-outism" position. Hearkening back to Warner's early theology of "love works unity," Brown took the position that those who professed faith in Christ for salvation already were members of the church of God, whether or not they left their denominational homes.[12] Brown argued that the spiritual unity of all Christians did not excuse their division. His basic position enabled people in the Church of God to take a far more positive attitude toward Christians of other traditions and persuasions. Through Brown's prolific editorial labor, Church of God people became increasingly familiar and comfortable with the idea that to "reach our hands in fellowship to every blood-washed one" meant fellowship with those saved in Christ wherever they may be found.

Thus the attitudes of the Church of God toward other churches are correlative to our two major self-understandings. A significant number of us, convinced that the church-historical exegesis is the proper method of interpreting the Scripture, maintain something of the spirit of "come-outism," although not in the same strident tones as those of earlier generations. Church of God people of this persuasion are very cautious in their relations with Christians of other traditions. Others of us have followed the line of thought running from Brown back through Reardon and Tasker. A more open stance toward other church groups characterizes persons of this persuasion. One caveat must be inserted here. In the Church of God it goes without saying that these are generalizations. An independent congregational polity insures that a wide spectrum of positions, some more open, others more closed, includes both points of view (and likely others, besides those) described here.

An Excursus on "Evangelicalism"

Early Church of God preachers and writers rejected all labels as means of self-identification. Even the term "Protestant" they regarded as unnecessary for New Testament Christians. The name *Christian* had been satisfactory for the followers of Jesus at Antioch, and early Church of God people saw no reason to depart from that scriptural standard. Over the years it has become acceptable within the Church of God movement, however, to designate itself as Protestant. In more recent years some in the Church of God, for reasons both theological and political, have taken to describing the Church of God as an evangelical communion. This is a historical and theological mistake.

Disregarding the notorious diversity among American Evangelicals,[13] one might identify the Church of God with the former because we share some common assumptions that typically identify them: (1) the authority of the Bible, (2) the necessity of personal conversion, and (3) the Great Commission to evangelism. To do so, however, overlooks a sequence of historic connections that links the Church of God with seventeenth century Pietists. The genealogy of Evangelicalism, on the other hand, can be traced back to those Protestant scholastic dogmatists who were contemporary with and often the target of Pietists, who criticized the excessive rationalism of the scholastics' theology.

The Pietists' complaint against the scholastics rested upon a set of epistemological assumptions that differed markedly from those held by the rationalist scholastics. Without traveling further afield here, suffice it to say that for Pietists the locus of assurance lay in the witness of the Spirit whereas for the scholastics it lay in the intellect's assent to sound doctrine. Indebted as it is to the Pietists through the Wesleys, the Church of God has understood religious knowledge to be available through the Word of Scripture but confirmed through the witness of the Spirit. It is, therefore, not at all uncommon to read testimonies in the prefaces of some of the movement's early books that claim the illumination (but stop short of *inspiration*) of the Holy Spirit for their work. So while many Church of God ministers and lay people share common social and political concerns with Evangelicals, on the whole it is a serious error to take that label, thereby risking the loss of one of the movement's central theological assumptions.

Major Emphases and the Future

Ecclesiology has been the central motif of theological reflection in the Church of God. Although arguable, it is fair to say that D. S. Warner subordinated his theology of sanctification to his ecclesiology; after all he did leave the holiness movement because to have remained a member would have compromised his understanding of the nature and organization of the church. At a later period in our history, after a decade of extensive institutionalization, the question of the organization of the church preoccupied the minds of various ministers. During the 1940s a serious schism occurred due to the perceptions of some that we had adopted the very organization and methods we originally had set out to protest. Ecclesiology obviously remained a central issue.

Particularly through the ministry of E. E. Byrum (1861-1942), *Gospel Trumpet* editor from 1895 to 1916, the doctrine of divine healing rose to a considerable prominence in the Church of God movement. The back page of the paper was devoted to testimonies of healing and arguments in support of the doctrine. But our claim that the marks of the true church were salvation of sinners, sanctification of believers, and divine healing of the sick raises a conjecture that one reason for the publication of those testimonies was to authenticate our claim to be a part of the restoration of the New Testament church. Similarly, the Gospel Trumpet Company published numerous polemical books, many of them by H. M. Riggle,[14] attacking premillenialists. Once again the Church of God's ecclesiology was implicated. If dispensationalist eschatologies were correct, then the Church of God's understanding of the church was not. I do not mean to suggest that divine healing and eschatology were not, or are not, regarded as important in their own right. But always the image of the church is somewhere close to the surface of the Church of God's theological consciousness. So here we are, now in our second century of existence. Once among the fastest growing churches in the United States, our rate of growth has begun declining to overall levels slightly above that of the general population. In 1992, North American membership totaled slightly more than 218,000; membership in the rest of the world exceeded 321,000. Once militantly opposed to institutional forms of education, we now sponsor five American colleges and a theological seminary. In those settings scholars struggle with the problems and issues that confront all Christians who live in this post-modern age. Once adamantly opposed to organization, the Church of God now possesses an elaborate network of agencies and commissions which have no ecclesial status but legal responsibility for millions of dollars in assets, a situation that sometimes bewilders lay people, clergy, and agency staffs alike.

All of these descriptions, and many more are possible, contribute to a situation pregnant with possibilities. How might those outside North America enrich the Church of God movement's ecclesiology and our understanding of what it means to be the people of God? How might our college professors appropriate the Church of God's theological commitments as resources for their own intellectual activity? How might the somewhat anomalous status of our agencies stimulate the development of a creative, biblically based polity?

Students in my courses sooner or later will hear me define a community as the conversation, extended through time, of the implications of its traditions. Borrowing from Stephen Sykes (1984, esp. 250-261) and others, it seems to me that the Church of God is an "essentially contested concept." Early "come-outers" commonly used the phrase, "I saw the church," to explain their decision to cast their lots with the Church of God movement. The struggle to see the church and then live up to that vision is the concept at the center of that conversation called the Church of God (Anderson, Ind.). Sometimes our passion for the church has escalated our conversation into an argument. We have argued with those outside the movement; we have argued with ourselves.

Even in this we have kept faith with a New Testament vision of the church where Paul once got in Peter's face over the status of Gentiles in the church. And why not? Few questions are of more pressing importance to those who name Jesus as their Master than this: What kind of people is God calling us to be in a world that knows not Jesus as its Lord? Peel away the layers of secondary concern and discussion and one finds Church of God preachers and writers constantly addressing that question in one fashion or another. And if that question was good enough for Peter and Paul, isn't it good enough for us?

Chapter One Notes

1. Standard histories of the Church of God include C. E. Brown, *When the Trumpet Sounded*, 1951, and John W. V. Smith, *The Quest for Holiness and Unity*, 1980.

2. Helpful accounts of the American holiness movement include Mel Dieter, *The Holiness Revival of the Nineteenth Century*, 1980; Charles E. Jones, *Perfectionist Persuasion: The Holiness Movement and American Methodism, 1867-1936*, 1974; and John Leland Peters, *Christian Perfection and American Methodism*, 1954.

3. Cf. *Bible Proofs of a Second Work of Grace*, 1880, and *Salvation, Present, Perfect, Now or Never*, n.d.

4. For a biography of Winebrenner see Richard Kern, *John Winebrenner: Nineteenth Century Reformer*, 1974.

5. John Winebrenner, *Doctrinal and Practical Sermons*. Published by the Authority of the General Eldership of the Church of God, 1868, 225.

6. Brown draws a close parallel here between Warner and Alexander Campbell of the Restorationist movement.

7. *Biblical Trace of the Church*

The church of the morning bright,	Arising the sun of day,
Like crystal so clear her light,	Disperses the night away,
Triumphant she knew no fears;	While popery quakes with fears;
In finest white linen dressed;	Shone dimly the gospel ray,
Pure holiness she possessed,	There followed a cloudy day;
Two hundred and seventy years.	Three hundred and fifty years.
The sun went down ere his time,	We welcome the evening light;
The moon also ceased to shine,	The gospel so clear and bright

Left Zion in bitter tears;	Breaks forth as in days of yore;
No star then, appeared in sight,	The mists are all cleared away,
Oh, long, dreary papal night!	All hail the supernal day!
Twelve hundred and sixty years.	The sun shall go down no more.

Chorus
Hell never can destroy the church,
Built by the Savior's hands,
Upon the Rock, the solid Rock,
Christ Jesus still she stands.

8. Those unfamiliar with this exegetical system will doubtless wonder about the method of calculating years and numbers. The critical numbers are 1,260 and 350. Revelation 11:2-3 refers to 42 months and 1,260 days. Reckoning 30 days to the month, the former equals the latter. Since a year is as a day in God's sight, if the papacy's rise to power is generally set as A.D. 270, and each of the 1,260 days is considered as a year and added to the former date, we arrive at the important year of 1530. By a similar method the 3 and 1/2 days mentioned in Rev. 11:9, 11 are interpreted to be 350 years and added to 1530. This calculation yields the date 1880, roughly the year in which the Church of God movement began its work.

9. Warner argued that anyone who continues membership in a denomination implicitly assents to the idea that there can be more than one church. Such a notion easily translated to the impossibility that more than one bride of Christ would make an adulterer of Jesus. Cf., *The Church of God*, n.d., 14-15.

10. 30-31. Warner concludes this tract on the church by appealing: "In the name of Jesus Christ, whose Word will soon judge us, we beseech all men to escape from all sin and sinners, from all sect clans, and sectish bands, and take refuge in Jesus Christ and his own church, which is the 'pillar and ground of the truth.' Amen." p. 31.

11. Cited in Robert H. Reardon, *The Early Morning Light*, 1979, 55.

12. Cf. especially the book Brown wrote for the Church of God golden jubilee, *A New Approach to Christian Unity*, 1931.

13. I once heard the fine sociologist of religion and Evangelical churchman David Moberg remark, "We cannot even agree whether to call ourselves evangelicals or Evangelicals." For a useful essay that explains the various applications of this term, see George Marsden's introductory essay in his *Evangelicalism and Modern America*, 1984: vii-xix.

14. Cf. *Christ's Kingdom and Reign*, 1918; *Christ's Second Coming and What Will Follow*, 1919; *Jesus Is Coming Again*, 1943; and *The Kingdom of God and the One Thousand Years' Reign*, 1899. Riggle was one of the Church of God movement's leading controversialists, especially on the topic of the millenium.

Witness ②

L
ess than twenty miles inland from the southeastern shore of Lake Michigan, the little village of Grand Junction sleeps on sandy soil where excellent blueberries grow. Local farmers ship their produce far and wide from this location. Railroad tracks run along the west edge of the village where a sign reminds residents of bygone days when Gospel Trumpet Company literature, not berries, was shipped from Grand Junction to the uttermost parts of the earth. In July, 1992, people of the Church of God in Michigan celebrated the centennial camp meeting of the Church of God movement at Grand Junction. That occasion set me to reflecting about the year of 1892 in the Church of God and how the movement in that year began to step more briskly into the wider world surrounding it.

1892 witnessed the births of at least two new camp meetings. The saints had been gathering for summer meetings at Bangor, Michigan, even before the Gospel Trumpet Company moved to Grand Junction from Williamston in 1886. But in 1892 the meeting moved to its present location on sixty acres of ground adjacent to Lester Lake. D. S. Warner purchased the site with the idea that it would make a fine setting for the annual camp meeting which, because of its association with the Trumpet company, rapidly grew into the largest of the numerous meetings held around the country. Thus it came to own the designation of the "general" camp meeting. It was on this ground that Warner also built the home that he, his wife "Frankie," and Warner's son Sidney occupied but a short while before Warner died in December, 1895. Three years later the Trumpet Company moved to Moundsville, West Virginia, but the saints who remained in Michigan continued to hold the camp meeting at Grand Junction, and they used the chapel on the grounds as their meeting place for regular weekly services during the remainder of the year.

From August 19 to 29 in that same year of 1892, Church of God people in western Pennsylvania founded the camp meeting that has met annually ever since near Emlenton. Known initially as the "Red Lion Camp Meeting," its founding organizers expected leading ministers G. T. Clayton and A. J. Kilpatrick to do most of the preaching. Calls for the meeting appeared in the *Trumpet* throughout the summer of 1892: "Brethren, come without fail; bring plenty of bedding and provision. Come to stay all the time." Those who were too poor to bring anything were nevertheless encouraged to attend because the Lord would provide. Reports from the meeting said that it was well attended and yielded much good fruit: thirteen were baptized and more than one hundred souls attended the ordinance services. *Gospel Trumpet* publisher E. E. Byrum visited Red Lion after stopping briefly at the camp meeting in Beaver Dam, Indiana. Byrum had felt impressed to visit the saints in the eastern United States and thus journeyed to Pennsylvania. Young Enoch got more than he expected at Red Lion, for there the young associate editor and publisher was ordained into the ministry.

Far to the west, in that same year of 1892, a former Methodist minister and professor of Greek at the University of Southern California, Benjamin F. Elliott, felt a call to preach to the Spanish-speaking people who lived near Santa Barbara, California. In the midst of his grief after the death of his wife, Elliott had cast his lot with the Church of God movement in the mid-1880s. After his call to cross-cultural mission, the college-educated Elliott immediately began teaching himself Spanish. But his call extended beyond the streets of Santa Barbara. By the end of the year he and his young son were in San Diego, awaiting the financial means that would open the way for them to sail to Ensenada, on the Baja Peninsula of Mexico. Who should they encounter during their wait but D. S. Warner, then on a preaching tour through the far west? As Elliott, his son, and their co-worker S. C. Shaw waited on the dock, Warner pressed into Elliott's hand the money necessary to purchase their passage to Mexico. In that moment cross-cultural mission was born among Church of God people. While the Elliott missionary party laid plans for Mexico, J. H. Rupert and W. J. Henry sailed across the Atlantic and opened a mission in England. They arrived at the northeast port of Liverpool and began work in that area and on the Wirral Peninsula. Later they were joined by George Achor and Lena Shoffner, but this mission also had its beginnings in the year of 1892.

In a real sense the entire Church of God movement was a missionary movement in the year 1892. Whether at camp meetings in

Benjamin F. Elliott, first cross-cultural missionary of the Church of God movement. Along with his young son and S. C. Shaw, Elliott distributed tracts and Bibles in the districts surrounding Ensenada, La Paz, and Mazatlan, Mexico. Altogether, he made four extended missionary tours of Mexico during the 1890s.

Grand Junction or Red Lion, street-preaching in Santa Barbara, passing out tracts in Ensenada, or witnessing in Liverpool, people in the movement then focused their efforts on getting the message out to those who had not heard God's call to holiness and unity. This marks the movement of 1892 as something of a departure from the churches of the surrounding religious world. Many of those churches distinguished the church from its missions; a church was settled, established, while missions were considered immature and necessarily dependent upon churches for their support and governance. More than a little paternalism shaped the distinction between church and mission.

Very little, if any, of the distinction between church and mission existed in the early years of the Church of God movement. Eventually this way of thinking made its way into our midst. But in 1892 that development still lay decades in the future. In 1892 men and women of the movement were "hurrying to and fro" with a message which saw the church in a fresh, vital way. To such people, captivated as they were by such a vision, distinctions between church and mission were irrelevant to the great task at hand. A message had to be proclaimed, whether in Michigan or Mexico, Pennsylvania or England. In 1892, new efforts by the Church of God led to the establishment of long-term ministries that in increasing numbers celebrate centennial anniversaries in places far and wide. No church launched these missions; rather they have been for a century now the product of the efforts of women and men who simply saw that there was work to be done. Seeing the task before them, they went out to do the best they could for a cause that transcended both divisions between Christians and the false distinctions that separate church and mission.

Vocation

Travel west-northwest from Nairobi for 150 miles and you will arrive in a district of Kenya's Western Province where the missionary work of the Church of God has flourished for more that sixty years. At Ingotse, a village in this region, stands Murray Memorial Church. This building honors the memory of James Murray and his wife, Ruth Fisher Murray, Church of God missionaries in the exciting and difficult early years of our work there.

Unlike Church of God missions in other parts of the world, the work in what then was called British East Africa was inaugurated by missionaries of other communions. A. W. Baker and his daughter, Mabel, of the South Africa Compound and Interior Mission, had never heard of the Church of God movement. But Mr. Baker sent staff members Henry and Gertrude Kramer to the United States in search of a church group that might take over the sponsorship of their mission at Kima. At Pomona, California in 1921, the Kramers met Abram and William Bixler, brothers of a stalwart Church of God family. The movement's mission in east Africa was born in that meeting. Little more that a year later the Missionary Board commissioned the Kramers, who had been Quakers, to return to Kima and head the work for which they had assumed responsibility. Ruth Fisher accompanied the Kramers to teach mis-

James Murray and Ruth Fisher Murray standing in front of a rural dwelling in British East Africa, now Kenya. Ruth Fisher came to Africa to teach the children of missionaries of the Church of God. There she met James Murray, himself a Salvation Army missionary who affiliated with the Church of God mission at Kima in 1921. They were married in 1925. Ruth Murray died in 1936 and James in 1940, both as a result of tropical illness.

sionary children at the station. All of a sudden, the Church of God had a growing African mission.

In 1921, a member of the Salvation Army, James Murray, went to East Africa as a missionary for that organization. Shortly after his arrival he affiliated himself with the infant Church of God mission there. Over the course of the next two or three years Ruth Fisher and James saw a great deal of each other, laboring as they did on the same field. In 1925 they were married. Then they transferred to Ingotse, a village of the Butsotso district, where they served the boys' school and worked in village evangelism.

The Murrays knew both the blessings and sacrifices of missionary service during the next decade. They helped the Church of God mission develop schools and clinics. They witnessed the rapid growth of the missionary staff. They rejoiced at the conversions of African tribes-people to Christianity. They were grateful when a young convert named Musa Eshipiri donated land for a new station at Mwhila. But the graves of three children, each of whom died in infancy, at Kima cemetery witness to the Murrays' heartache. Then, in 1936, Mrs. Murray fell desperately ill with typhoid fever. The disease overpowered Ruth, and James buried her next to their children. Four years later the body of James Murray was laid to rest in the same cemetery after he succumbed to a particularly virulent form of malaria called blackwater fever. Although the Murrays did not labor in quest of human recognition, the Kenyan church appropriately honored their service by naming the church at Ingotse after Ruth and James.

As a boy I was often told how missionaries made great sacrifices to carry the gospel to people who had never heard the name of Jesus. In our home and in the church we considered missionaries to be contemporary heroes and heroines of the faith, sometimes even martyrs. In those days the news that Auca Indians had killed five missionaries in the South American jungle only confirmed the heroic stature of missionaries in our eyes.

Of course, such esteem frequently embarrassed missionaries, who considered themselves ordinary people simply responding to God's call upon their lives. The same is true of our contemporaries on the mission field. And yet, while their service may not bear the tragic dimensions of the story of Ruth and James Murray, the sacrifices of modern day missionaries should not be minimized. Because of their calling they do give up goods like friendship and family for the sake of a higher good.

The Latin word for calling is *vocatio*. From it we get our word "vocation." Unfortunately this term has come to be little more than a fancy word signifying what we do for a living. We ought to lament the destruction of a good word in this way. For "job," "career," and "vocation" do not mean the same thing; they are not synonyms for "work." It is unthinkable that Ruth and James considered their labor a job, or that when they moved to Ingotse they were making a "career move." Missionary service was their vocation. It is not that they were missionaries that distinguishes the Murrays' service as vocation. Rather, their characters were of such a quality that they saw their lives as gifts of time and space of the service of God and neighbor. That vision means that they would have had vocations whether they had been missionaries or workers in the factory just up the street in Anytown, USA. That their lives displayed in such an extraordinary manner their vision of life as vocation should not be allowed to obscure from our sight the realization that we too may have more than jobs or careers, but probably not without some cost.

Missionary Presence

On June 27, 1925, the Cunard liner, R.M.S. *Carmania*, steamed out of New York harbor, bound for Queenstown, Ireland. One of the passengers on board was starting the first leg of a trip around the world. This was no sightseeing trip, but a missionary journey. The traveler intended to visit mission stations in Europe, Asia, Africa, and Australia, making inspections, encouraging missionaries who had not been home for years, meeting native churches, and preaching at worship services and young people's meetings. The traveler's name was Charles J. Blewitt, pastor of the Church of God congregation housed in the New York missionary home.

Blewitt left behind his wife, Anna, and their six children. He faithfully wrote to them over the course of his year-long absence. Anna saved the entire correspondence, which was mailed from places like Paris, Beirut, Port Said, Mombasa, Calcutta, Nanking, Tokyo and Sydney. The file of letters became Blewitt's travel diary, and it now is a wonderful record of places, events, and people of the early days of the Church of God movement's missionary effort. Even more, Blewitt's correspondence and his trip itself reveals something of the sense of importance that the movement attached to missionary work.

C.J. Blewitt could be counted among the movement's leaders in 1925. Fifty-two years old, he had been in the ministry since he was seventeen. Anna Blewitt, the assistant pastor of the New York Missionary Home, was herself an ordained minister. Charles sat on a missionary board that included such prominent names as E. E. Byrum, J. W. Phelps, F. G. Smith, Bessie Byrum, J. D. Smoot, H.M. Riggle, A. F. Gray, E. A. Reardon and J. W. Byers. This board needed first-hand information from the mission field, so Blewitt took the courageous and sacrificial step of sailing around the world to encourage missionaries and congregations as well as gather reports. Only voluntary contributions funded his trip. Blewitt took pains to tell anyone and everyone that no missionary offering monies were used to defray his expenses.

I suppose Blewitt was sensitive to the criticism that he was off on a yearlong junket, but one need not read many of his letters before appreciating the difficulty and hazards of travel only sixty-five years ago. Americans today take it rather for granted that any place in the world they will find someone who speaks English. That surely was not the case in 1925, thereby rendering communication much more problematic. Blewitt sailed on ships that answered distress signals from other vessels whose "wireless" equipment had malfunctioned. He rode many a night train where the "sleeping berth" was the bench on which he was seated. The only bedding available was the pillow and blanket he carried with him. To be sure, Blewitt saw wonderful and exotic sights in some of the worlds far-flung places, from the British Museum to Himalayan gorges and the Taj Mahal. But sight-seeing was not his purpose. The inconvenience of the travel and a year away from loved ones was a price too expensive for a mere sightseeing trip.

Reading through Blewitt's letters, one finds nearly all the names of the first great wave of Church of God missionaries who went out in the decades between 1900 and 1920. The Crose family was in Syria (now Lebanon) and the Neffs in Egypt. In British East Africa the Kramers, Murrays, and Baileys had opened the mission that was the apple of Blewitt's eye. About the Kenyan situation he wrote, "I have not found a more desirable spot on the whole missionary field. The beauty of the scenery, the healthfulness of the climate, the easy language, the teachable natives, the capable missionaries offset the many unpleasant things which every mission field has in common." Back in New York, Anna Blewitt surely shared this optimism with Charles and Twyla Ludwig, who were then at the missionary home awaiting departure for the East African mission. Blewitt hoped that the Ludwigs would open an infirmary. They did in fact, and their efforts began the Church of God medical mission in Kenya. Blewitt also asked his wife to take Mrs. Ludwig aside privately and tell her she would need to learn how to treat the sores associated with syphilis. The work had its grim side, too.

Other well-known missionary names appear in Blewitt's letters. In India many of these names belong to national leaders like Roy, Moses, and Das. The Indian church still mourned the loss of A.D. Khan, who had died three years before Blewitt's arrival. Faith Stewart and Josephine McCrie had been laboring at the Shelter in Cuttack. Mona Moors included a note to Anna Blewitt in one of Charles' letters home. He also wrote of the Taskers, the Hunnexes and Daisey Maiden in China, Adam Miller and Axchie Bolitho in Japan.

Away from home for a full year, C. J. Blewitt sailed through the Golden Gate in the late spring of 1926. His heart and mind carried a wealth of information and concern about the people and places he had visited. He had left among them a good bit of himself in the bargain—preaching, teaching, listening, encouraging. His journey displayed the Christian virtue of presence. He had his worries about the mission work, but he believed in the honest effort being made by all concerned. They were doing the best they could, he said. One gets the impression that so was he.

The Gospel Van

The River Dee rises in Wales and runs east many miles before turning north toward the Irish Sea. Just before meeting the sea, the Dee runs through the charming old city of Chester, whose name is the English form of the Latin word for "fort." The river's banks have been traveled by Roman soldiers, Celtic and Viking warriors, and Norman bishops. On August 15, 1897, a different sort of foot-prints graced the banks of this lovely old river, for at Chester on that day missionaries of the Church of God movement conducted a service of baptism.

The Church of God mission in England began in the move-ment's very early days. In those first years of missionary work, missions took the form of the person who felt burdened to carry the

The Gospel Van

Word to souls who had not yet heard it. In 1892, the first Church of God missionary, Benjamin F. Elliot left California for Mexico. Before the end of that same year J. H. and Hattie Rupert sailed for England.

The Rupert missionary party landed in Liverpool. Characteristically, they started their gospel work on the spot. The Wirral peninsula, the western shore of which is bounded by the Dee's estuary, became the focus of the group's activity. The Ruperts held missions in Chester and Hoylake, Warrington and Birkenhead. Birkenhead became the center of operations, with a mission home rented at 94 Chester Street. For several reasons the

Ruperts labored in stony ground. The English viewed themselves as a Christian society, but the English church was benignly neglected by the nobility and genteel society and ignored by the working classes. Decades earlier D. L. Moody had conducted successful revivals in England, but the sight of the saints baptizing eleven new converts in the River Dee prompted mostly the curious to come out and watch; such things simply were not done in England. Rupert estimated that a crowd of some 5,000 people watched the baptisms. The crowd was not composed of worshipers—only curious onlookers.

The scope of the Ruperts' task nearly overwhelmed them. He compared it to a single couple attempting to harvest ten thousand acres of wheat with a cradling scythe and rake. Moreover, the missionary labor often had to compete with income-generating work. J. H. Rupert would often work "with his hands," as he put it, for three months or longer on a schedule where the days were occupied with work to put food on the table and evenings were spent preaching the gospel. Rupert's letters to the Gospel Trumpet always appealed to his readers, hoping that some would share his burden, answer the call and join him and his wife in England. Because England was a world-wide transportation center, missionaries bound for the Middle East and Asia often interrupted their journeys to assist the Ruperts for brief periods of time. So, for example, on his way to India, Gorham Tufts stayed with the Ruperts and helped them with the work. Others who joined the English mission were George and Mary Achor, W. J. Henry, J. W. Daugherty, and Lena Shoffner.

As in the United States, so in England the *Gospel Trumpet* workers placed a premium on mobility. Getting the message to as many as possible was the highest priority. In consideration of this, Rupert hit on an idea reminiscent of the *Floating Bethel* and the *Gospel Ark*. Rupert created the *Gospel Van*. Built in July, 1895, this horse-drawn wagon contained living quarters and cooking facilities for the evangelistic company who drove it about the English countryside. The van also stored, inevitably, gospel literature that was distributed free to the crowd that gathered wherever it stopped. Now the Ruperts and their associates could take the message of salvation, holiness, and unity down any English street or lane. Before they reached hailing distance, the lettering on the wagon's side announced their message: "Non-Sectarian Gospel Van." "Tracts and Pamphlets Free." "Christ the Only Remedy."

By some standards the labors of the Ruperts and other missionaries to England might be harshly judged as having produced no great results. A small congregation still meets in Birkenhead, and efforts to gather a flock in Liverpool also continue. The congregation in London is the result of much more recent missionary efforts and is not historically related to the Rupert's work in northwest England. The numbers resulting from that mission are not especially large, but it is no small thing to have been a congregation of faithful Christians for a century, as the Birkenhead church can testify. Many North American congregations cannot say as much.

Another standard can be put forward to assess the Rupert's English mission. That standard is the intrinsic value of this testimony, written at Birkenhead more than twenty years after the "Gospel Van" first rolled into town.

> The Lord in his wisdom has allowed me to pass through some very deep waters, and my soul has been tested in the heated fires of trial. Presumably it is because of this I now enjoy the constant pleasure and thrills of his love in my heart. I expect to increase more and more, for I long to be more like Jesus, who was so meek and lowly in heart, and such a beautiful example for all men (*G.T.,* W. Hopwood, 1916:14).

No Little Plans

The World Conference of the Church of God convened in Wiesbaden, Germany July 19-21, 1991. The meeting's very name sets us to meditating on the world-wide dimensions of the Church of God movement. Around the world, more than a half-million souls are considered to be affiliated with the Church of God (Anderson). More than half that number live in countries other than the United States and Canada. One hundred thousand of that larger section live in Kenya alone. Statistics are impressive, but they are mere numbers. Behind the impressive statistics we find the stories

Nora Siens Hunter (1873-1951), founder of the National Women's Home and Foreign Missionary Society of the Church of God, now known as the Women of the Church of God. An ordained minister, during her life Mrs. Hunter served as an evangelist in the Midwest and Eastern United States, a worker in the Sebastian and Chloe Michels' Children's Home, and a pastor in Los Angeles.

of men and women. Of course, no single person can be credited with the movement's growth around the world. A vision of the church beyond division has fired the hearts and imaginations of countless missionaries at home and abroad. Nevertheless, some faces stand out; one in particular belongs to Nora S. Hunter.

After 1932 and the organization that year of the Woman's Home and Foreign Missionary Society, Nora Hunter could most likely be found on a train bound for yet another American town or city. She traveled at what seems a nonstop pace in those early days of the society of which she was the founding president. The new organization had to be introduced at camp meetings and ministers' meetings. State and local societies needed to be organized. A great deal of work was necessary all over the country, and Nora Hunter was the woman for the job.

Nora Siens was born in a one-room house on the Kansas prairie in August, 1873. Her father, a Civil War veteran, and her mother held a deep faith that nurtured their family through a series of tragedies. First Nora's mother, Anna, died. This was followed by the deaths of Nora's infant sister and her younger brother, George. Robert Siens could not care for his two remaining children, so he placed them in an orphanage for the children of war veterans.

At the age of eighteen, Nora, now living with relatives near Galesburg, Kansas, heard S. G. Bryant preach messages about salvation and the oneness of all Christians. Nora responded to these sermons and offered her heart and life to the service of this vision. First she traveled with Dr. and Mrs. Bryant, assisting them in their evangelistic efforts. By summer 1893, Nora Siens had become a member of the Gospel Trumpet family in Grand Junction, Michigan. At the age of nineteen she joined in the evangelistic work of people like D. S. and Frankie Warner, G. T. and Lizzie Clayton, W. J. Henry and others. In 1896, Nora married Clarence Hunter, and they formed an evangelistic company themselves. Nora was the more gifted leader of the two, and she assumed the larger share of the responsibilities.

The two ministers undertook evangelistic campaigns all across the United States, but in the late 1920s Nora made a trip that dramatically changed the focus of her attention. Through her brother's generosity, Nora sailed to Europe and the Holy Land. During the course of her travels Nora saw firsthand the spiritual and economic plight of thousands of men and women, boys and girls. She also saw firsthand the hardships endured by many missionaries because the Missionary Board lacked sufficient funds to pay them their "allowance," as salaries then were termed. With the coming of the Depression, already short allowances were reduced—more than once. Nora had heard stories of this problem, but in 1929 she saw it with her own eyes. She returned home determined to do something. Two years transpired before her determination took definite shape.

Nora Hunter's vision began taking on specific form during the 1931 Anderson Camp Meeting. While there she had a conversation with Evelyn Nichols-Roy and Grace Henry. Nora shared with her two friends her vision of a national organization of women of the Church of God. Mrs. Nichols-Roy and Mrs. Henry instantly affirmed Nora's idea. The next day about two hundred women attended a hastily called meeting for the purpose of further exploration into the organization of a woman's missionary society. One year later, after working at a pace that would have fatigued many a younger person, Nora Hunter assumed the presidency of the newly organized National Woman's Home and Foreign Missionary Society of the Church of God.

At age fifty-eight Nora Hunter was about to embark on a second career that would find her criss-crossing the nation in behalf of her beloved work and its great cause. She possessed unbelievable enthusiasm, energy, and vision for her task. When the speaking, publishing, and correspondence paused, Mrs. Hunter used the time knitting yet another afghan to be used as a gift or perhaps as an item for barter in exchange for the support of another new idea. She continued in her assignment until 1948, when she at last stepped into retirement and a well-deserved rest.

According to John W. V. Smith, Mrs. Hunter often quoted the following lines of Daniel Burnham: "Make no little plans. They have no magic to stir men's blood."[1] The woman's society surely was no small plan, and it entertained no small vision of its own. The society was determined that the Missionary Board's financial problems would not be allowed to force the recall of any missionary. Largely through the woman's society efforts and their grass-roots "Penny-a-Day" program, allowances were increased and no missionaries were forced to leave their stations.

In July of 1991, red, yellow, black and white peoples of the world gathered at Wiesbaden, Germany. It is not a very great strain on one's credulity to suggest that a line of faith might be drawn from Nora Hunter and the women who, like her, made no small plans, to believers from any one of a dozen countries, gathered in a fellowship around the world so vast.

Press On

The day before Valentine's Day, 1986, at Santa Cruz, California, Daisy Maiden Boone, age 102, departed this life. Anyone born in the nineteenth century and who lives until almost the close of the twentieth will have seen a great many wonders. Consider the many inventions of the last century. How many objects, not even *imagined* in 1890 when Daisy was a seven year old girl, now litter American households?

Anyone who lives more than one hundred years experiences a great many changes. But Daisy Maiden Boone was not just anyone. During the course of her extraordinary life she homesteaded 160 acres of eastern Washington farmland and taught school. After her conversion and association with the Church of God movement, her activities turned ever-increasingly toward spiritual matters. She visited the sick and women in prison. Among several other young people, Daisy lived and worked in the Seattle missionary home. Along with training for evangelistic work, these young people fanned out across Seattle and the neighboring regions selling subscriptions to the *Gospel Trumpet*, ten weeks' issues for ten cents. During those years Daisy formed friendships that enriched her long life.

Daisy's parents, Emory and Molly Maiden, had moved their family west from southwestern Virginia to Washington in 1889, having sojourned along the way for a few years in Douglas County, Kansas. Emory fell to work bringing under cultivation a section of farmland near Creston. Good, decent, hard-working people, the Maidens were not particularly religious.

Emory's younger brother, Victor, had also moved out to Washington and farmed wheat near his brother's place. A little band of flying messengers led by Fred Jacobsen came through Creston and held meetings there. Victor's wife, Florence, attended these meetings against her husband's staunch Southern Baptist objections. Victor changed his tune when Florence came home from the meetings saying that the prayers of the saints had been answered and that she had been healed of the tuberculosis that had so badly afflicted her. In only a very short time Victor became a minister of the Church of God. In 1906, Victor and Florence moved their family to Assam, India; God had called them to missionary service. Within two years of their arrival in India, all of the members of the Victor and Florence Maiden family were dead of malaria and tropical disease.

> Before he fell ill, Daisy's uncle Victor, now the sole surviving member of his family, wrote her a letter in which he said, I can only say, PRESS ON. There is nothing but victory ahead to those who will fight, and the way gets brighter and better all the time. Oh, my soul sings for joy unto the Lord for his great goodness to us. There is a glorious end to this race, so let us not weary in well-doing (Fox 1987: 18-19).

Prior to his family's departure for India, Victor had hoped that someone from Emory's family would be saved and come to see the church even as he had. Daisy spent the summer with her aunt and uncle in 1906, and it was there, while attending a camp meeting near Creston, that she experienced conversion.

Daisy did, in fact, press on. She felt called to gospel work and formed a friendship with Belle Watson while living in the Seattle missionary home. Later Daisy moved across the Cascade mountains to her home region and took up residence in the Spokane missionary home. She found herself drawn particularly to those who were down and out or shut in by affliction or prison bars.

Daisy and Belle both supported themselves by teaching school. That left their summers free for evangelistic work. They accompanied Rev. and Mrs. Daniel Rice in the rugged district around Montesano, Washington. Soon both women felt called to full-time ministry. Belle answered first and moved to Anderson, where she joined the Gospel Trumpet family. Daisy followed her in 1914.

The same year that Daisy joined Belle in Anderson, William and Gloria Hunnex, missionaries to China, returned to America on furlough. The work in China was vast, and the Hunnexes sought help. The success of their mission depended on their return to China with some new missionaries, especially single women who could visit Chinese homes. Daisy and Belle answered the call. In 1916, in the company of the Hunnexes, they sailed through the Golden Gate to China.

Daisy Maiden served two terms in China. Sandwiched in between was a teaching assignment at Pacific Bible College in its first year of operations. While there she herself comprised half the faculty. In 1951 she married Samuel Boone, whom she had first met at the Spokane missionary home decades earlier.

Space limitations permit only the briefest of sketches of Daisy Maiden Boone's extraordinary life. How very much one could say about her. But among all that could be said, it strikes me that her life was marked in an unusual way by friendship and constancy. Consider the significance of friendship in Daisy's spiritual development. Her Christian discipleship, her understanding of who she was in relation to God and the world hinged on the presence of friends like her uncle Victor and Belle Watson. By "friend" I mean a relationship far more significant than our modern phrase "just a friend" can hope to signify. The friend I have in mind is the rare person who becomes another self to us, who helps us see ourselves in light of what is truly important. Such friendships share a common pursuit of the good. Victor and Belle shared with Daisy a common quest for God.

Daisy's life was also marked by constancy. The moral philosopher Alasdair MacIntyre describes constancy as similar to patience, but more than merely patient. Constancy implies a gentle certainty, a reliability amid all the vicissitudes of life. Daisy Maiden Boone's life displayed the virtue of constancy. It would seem to be the case that friendship and constancy are among the most important virtues of a flourishing life of Christian discipleship. They sustained Daisy Maiden Boone through a century.

Telling Stories, Shaping Faith

One of the larger sections of the Archives of the Church of God contains copies of all the curriculum, in all age groups, published by the Church of God movement. Even a casual observer of these shelves can hardly fail to be impressed by the sheer size of this collection, for they hold more than 200 bound volumes of Sunday School curriculum. Even at that these volumes do not include the numberless posters and teachers kits that also have been produced as teacher resources. The sheer bulk of all this curriculum testifies to the importance that the movement has assigned to the ministry of Christian education.

The *Primary Teacher's Quarterly* for 1927 opens with an introduction prepared by the curriculum writer, a woman named Anna Koglin. Thirty-five years of age, Koglin had been in the ministry since 1913. She already had served God and the church in some unusual and exciting ways. Anna had grown up on the prairies of extreme northwestern Minnesota. That religious landscape was divided among Lutherans and Roman Catholics, since it had been settled largely by Scandinavian and German immigrants. Anna's family could be numbered among the latter, and thus her early religious instruction was Lutheran.

As a young woman Anna encountered the Church of God movement and was impressed by its message of holiness and unity. She became a "come-outer," but the vision of a spiritually unified church compelled her to offer her own life in the realization of that vision. She journeyed to St. Paul Park, Minnesota, and joined the little band hard at work publishing the message of the Church of God movement among Scandinavian-speaking peoples. She also worked as a *colporteur*, a person who traveled about the countryside selling or giving away religious literature. This was potentially hazardous work, but young Anna discounted the danger. Later she journeyed to Anderson, where for many years she taught in the language department at Anderson College. Clearly, Anna Koglin knew firsthand the love of God and could respond to that love by giving God the only appropriate gift—her life, fully and without any reservation.

I mention all of this because Anna Koglin told the teachers who used the curriculum she had written that it was intended to impress children with the idea of God's love for them. The point of the lessons was that children come to know, personally come to experience, God's love. Anna regarded this experiential knowledge as much more important than that the students amass great quantities of information. Now she did not mean to suggest that the teacher's job was simply to say "God loves you." Rather, the teacher was to love students and tell them the great stories of the Bible, which make the point of God's free and gracious love for us.

The students in one of my theology seminars were intrigued by two different notions of the word *faith*: the faith that believes and the faith that is believed. The former refers to faith's experiential dimension, the latter to the narrative structure that helps us to know that which we believe. Both are important aspects of faith, and both notions seem to have been employed instinctively by Anna Koglin in her curriculum writing. The stories we learn shape the faith by which we come to God. Neither the stories nor the faith that acts upon them can be neglected in the church's educational ministry.

The reason why we dare not neglect either aspect of faith is because, when you come right down to it, very little that the church does is without some dimension of Christian education. Better said, the whole entity we call church is Christian education. People who come to God in faith for the forgiveness of sin are only beginning to be made disciples. Christian education is the whole enterprise of shaping that new life in Christ, telling the stories of the people of God that shape the faith by which the babe in Christ believes. Christian education is not merely informative or catechetical; it shapes our characters as disciples of the Master. As such, it is the ministry not of some segment of the church, but the whole church. Anna Koglin understood that, which is why she exhorted her readers to tell the old, old story and love their students. Thus they too might come to experience God's love, a love she knew in the depths of her soul.

A Land of Suffering Women

Southwest of Calcutta and the mouths of the Ganges River in the Indian state of Orissa, lies the city of Cuttack. Not far from the Bay of Bengal, this city has been a site of Church of God movement gospel work for more than seventy-five years. The centerpiece of this work is known simply as The Shelter. Women have been the focus and laborers of this home and school for young Indian girls.

"*Suttee*" is the word for the Indian practice, outlawed by the British Raj in the nineteenth century, of burning alive a deceased man's widow on his funeral pyre. One would naturally think that the abolition of this custom would improve the lot of Indian women; however that did not prove to be the case. In fact, the lives of many women in India actually led to great suffering after *suttee* was prohibited.

In the very early dawn of Church of God missions, men and women of the Church of God in the United States and Canada offered themselves for service in India. The early women missionaries, E. Faith Stewart and Josephine McCrie among them, were particularly touched by the plight of Indian women, especially those who had been widowed. For the abolition of *suttee* had made the lives of widows a living death.

In 1916 Josephine McCrie estimated that some twenty-five million widowed women lived in India. Custom forbade marriage outside of one's caste, and it also encouraged the practice of child marriage. This combination meant that many Indian widows were twelve years old and even younger.

Local versions of popular Hinduism believed that the child-widow and the childless widow must have been very wicked in a former life to have such calamity befall them in this one. Their communities often, therefore, considered them accursed. The lower the caste to which the woman belonged, the more intensely her community ostracized her. The movement's missionaries worked extensively among peoples of India's lower castes. So women like McCrie, Stewart and Mona Moors became familiar with some of the worst cases of Indian widowhood.

Her head shaved, her garments coarse, shorn of all jewelry or ornamentation, the Indian widow was permitted only one meal per day and required to fast twice a month. Small wonder that Faith Stewart reported in the *Trumpet* that the sixteen-year-old wife of an Indian man drowned herself when her husband suffered a critical illness. The teen-age wife preferred death to life as a widow.

Josephine McCrie served as a missionary of the Church of God in India from 1904 to 1946. She was involved primarily with The Shelter in Cuttack, the institution founded by A. D. Khan for widowed or orphaned young women and girls. In 1941 McCrie married George Tasker, himself one of the movement's early missionaries in India.

Against this sad, sad backdrop Indian converts to Christianity and North American missionaries cooperated in efforts to care for some of India's children. The Church of God mission in India had begun when John A. D. Khan and others asked E. E. Byrum to send them literature about the movement. Gorham Tufts, of the Chicago Open Door Mission, subsequently traveled to India with a gift of over two thousand dollars for famine relief. While there, Tufts visited Lahore where he contacted Robert and Laura Jarvis, who had opened an independent faith-mission orphanage. Within a few years the movement took over sponsorship of this work.

The Lahore orphanage operated for more than two decades before closing. But before it shut its doors, Khan started another children's home, this one in Cuttack. The Shelter opened in 1914. Faith Stewart and Khan's two sisters-in-law, Sonat and Molini Mundul provided the staff for this venture. In 1917 the Indian church purchased seven acres of land for the project, and by 1919 the main building was constructed. In that same year a girls' elementary school was begun.

In 1916 The Shelter housed twenty-five girls, and the numbers grew rapidly as workers joined the home. Saturday Bible classes began. Each girl was sponsored personally by someone from the Church of God far across the seas. But early success was dimmed by deaths due to cholera and typhoid fever. Stewart wrote in the summer of 1916 that she wished for a little time away up in the hills where she might escape the torrid heat of the Indian summers. But she remained in Cuttack because "there is no one to stay with the work." Soon Josephine McCrie joined The Shelter staff, eventually becoming the home's superintendent.

What did these women think of this work to which they were called in a land so far away from home and a culture so different from theirs? Faith Stewart answered that question for herself and all the others who have given of themselves at The Shelter:

"When we think of what the future of these children would have been if they had not found shelter in this home, we are made to thank God for the privilege of being here" (*G.T.* 1916: 12).

Urban Mission

Missionary publications in the Church of God movement have a long history. The earliest of them, *Missionary Herald*, appeared in January, 1910. D. O. Teasley edited the monthly along with his good friend, Associate Editor George P. Tasker. The *Herald* published articles of interest to missions both foreign and domestic. Contributing editors for the year 1911 mailed articles to the *Herald* from addresses as exotic as Chinkiang, China, and as hometown as Alexandria, Indiana. The editors considered Birmingham, Alabama, a mission field as needy as Assam, India.

Late in 1911 and early in 1912 the plight of women in urban America received the focused attention of the *Missionary Herald* through a pair of articles written by a woman named Florence Roberts. Their style is elegantly simple and straightforward, but just under the surface smolders a passion for what then were known as "rescue homes." Matching this passion is an equally intense concern for a church that seemed to neglect its responsibility for such homes. Actually, "neglect" may be too generous a word to describe the attitude of a disinterested church that wanted to keep the members of these homes "in their place" because they were not the sort desired by the church's fashionable members. Roberts' first article is a tour in word-pictures of a rescue home. A home worker shows readers the home through the eyes and comments of an imaginary visitor. At first the visitor is surprised at the home's appearance; rather than institutionally cold and formidable, it is altogether pleasant and inviting. In this the home fits right in with the neighborhood houses. But the home's neighbors are unhappy with its presence. "The majority would rejoice if we would move. It has never been popular to neighbor with us, and yet the best thing for their [i.e., the neighbors] spiritual welfare is transpiring right in their midst, if they would but admit it"(1911: 371).

In the language of her day, Roberts refers to the home's residents as "inmates." She also calls them her daughters and the whole group "our family." The young women, and they all are described as "young," have come to this home from all sorts of victimization: alcohol and drugs, crime, vice, abuse. The living conditions in the home are anything but elegant. Although neat and clean, the kitchen larders are not amply stocked. Late on Saturday night butchers donate only the meat that will taint if kept over Sunday. A barrel holds broken crackers sent over from a biscuit factory.

Along with broken crackers and beef on the verge of spoiling, the girls who come to this home find another pantry overflowing with love, patience, kindness, and prayer. Matron, staff and inmates—this family—all sit at the same table. They eat the same simple fare. They live by the same Spirit.

About the same time as Roberts' imaginary visitor prepares to leave, the home's phone rings. The matron announces that another girl will soon arrive. The "girls" all join in the preparations for this stranger's welcome. One thinks of the verse in Luke about killing the fatted calf and making ready the feast to celebrate the return of another lost child.

Florence Roberts' second article has a hard edge on it. In the first she flashes her impatience with those who could support the home but refuse or give only minimally to the work. The sequel reveals a deeper impatience with a church that wishes to "do something" for the girls of the home—but only from a distance, without personal contact or involvement.

Jenny and Laura, two rescue home inmates attend the worship services of an otherwise unidentified "fashionable church." Laura has already been converted; Jenny has not but is trying to change her life. On a visit to the fashionable church's Sunday school class, Laura testifies to her conversion and makes clear the kind of life

The Hispanic-American Church of God at San Antonio, Texas in 1937. Mariano Tafolla stands second from the extreme right. The sign names him as the evangelist in a revival campaign with meetings every night except Saturday.

from which she was saved. Soon the pastor of this church learns of this testimony and asks the home's matron to visit him. During their awkward conversation the minister gives $5 to the rescue mission and then asks that the inmates not return to his church. The matron returns the minister's money to him and walks home. The girls are saddened to learn the true character of the church that would give money but not love—all of them but Jenny, who decides that she would rather leave the home and return to her former life than associate with the Christians of the fashionable church. The girls search for Jenny, but she is never again seen.

Florence Roberts concluded this true story by warning those who profess to be followers of Jesus' way, yet by their hardheartedness cause such little ones as Jenny to stumble. Then she quoted Luke 17:1-2: "It were better for you that a millstone were hanged about your neck, and that you be cast into the depths of the sea." Back in 1911 people told things as they saw them (1912:15).

God Gave the Increase

Neither the Puritans of Massachusetts Bay nor the Pilgrims of Plymouth colonies thought to set aside an *annual* day to offer thanks for the blessings that God had bestowed upon them. For those people, "to fix thanksgiving to a mechanical revolution of the calendar would be folly: who can say [with certainty] that in November there will be that for which thanks should be uttered rather than lamentation" (Miller 1961:19).

Early New England colonists kept days of humiliation as well as thanksgiving. A good harvest signaled God's favor and for that the colonists gave thanks. Drought, shipwreck, disease, or marauding Indians signaled God's displeasure with the people of New England. To such calamities they responded with days of fasting and humiliation, beseeching the Lord's forgiveness and the restoration of God's favor. I should not be surprised to learn that New England fasted and humbled itself more often than it gave thanks. Besides, as Perry Miller observes, "By the time ceremonial gratitude can be channelized into an annual festival, calculated in advance, society is rewarding its own well-doing, not acknowledging divine favor" (19).

Thousands of miles southwest of the rolling Massachusetts hills Hispanic settlers had built colonies some twenty years before English-speaking people stepped off the Mayflower. American history is dominated by the culture of our eastern seaboard, and we have forgotten—if we ever knew—of other ethnic contributions to our cultural and religious heritage. While the rest of the culture celebrates the New England tradition, it might be appropriate for us to reflect on the Hispanics, here before the Pilgrims, and their latter-day descendants who are part of the Church of God movement.

In 1921 Mariano F. Tafolla, a Mexican-American minister of the

Church of God, opened a Spanish-speaking mission in San Antonio, Texas. Tafolla, forty-six, and his wife, Eloise, were the parents of ten children. Having entered the ministry about 1903, Tafolla learned about the Church of God through a copy of the *Gospel Trumpet*. How often could that sentence describe the means of the movement's expansion in the first quarter of the twentieth century? Tafolla's work at San Antonio began through an invitation to speak to Mexican-American farm workers. His open air preaching among them paved the way for a Spanish language camp meeting on the Medina River at Somerset. The San Antonio congregation benefited from Mariano Tafolla's work for twenty-six years.

A year before the opening of the Spanish congregation at San Antonio, the General Ministerial Assembly authorized the founding of the Board of Church Extension and Home Missions. The first home missionary to receive the financial support of this board was none other than Marion Tafolla, thereby inaugurating a continuing relationship between the board and the Hispanic work.

Shortly after the beginning of the San Antonio church, Hispanic congregations started in other Texas towns. Tafolla's work and the Medina camp meeting soon led to a new church at Somerset. In 1933 L. Y. Janes started a congregation at Corpus Christi. Given the manner in which the movement spread through the medium of the written word, one can easily understand Janes' wish for a Spanish-language press. Out of his desire the Christian Triumph Publishing Company and its paper, *La Trompeta*, were born.

Support for the growing Hispanic work was strong. Church of God people in Anderson organized the Spanish Evangelical Association as a subsidiary of the Gospel Trumpet Company. The Association published another Spanish language paper, *La Verdad Apostolica*, and it supported the beginning of a congregation in Los Angeles. A. T. Maciel opened a work there in 1931, and six years later the Board of Church Extension and Home Missions assisted the congregation in securing its own building. Pastor Maciel served this church, known as Belvedere Church of God, until 1950.

In 1954 Church of God Hispanics organized the Spanish-American *Concilio*, an organization to assist in plans for the growth of established congregations and the planting of new ones. The *Concilio* also addresses matters such as the education and training of future Hispanic church leaders.

None of the growth and development of the Hispanic Church of God could have been foreseen when a man named Ball handed Mariano Tafolla a copy of the *Gospel Trumpet*. The time, talent, energy, and finances of many people have contributed to that growth. But, even in unlimited quantities, human dedication could not guarantee the success of that enterprise. Planting and watering must be undertaken within the care of God, who gives the increase. When we forget that, or when we think that our planning has covered every contingency, we no longer need to thank God; we need only congratulate ourselves. Seems like idolatry, doesn't it?

Performing the Scripture

From its earliest days the Gospel Trumpet Company incorporated the idea of family in its thought and practice. The handful of men and women who labored long hours to publish the *Gospel Trumpet* were known to them, and us, as the "Trumpet Family", and this reference was more than mere rhetoric. Family-like relationships characterized the workers' dealings with one another. The Trumpet home manager and matron took on the role of surrogate parents to workers, many of whom left their homes as teen-agers to join the publishing work.

Some adult Trumpet family members were estranged from their own families, and others, like Mother Sarah Smith, left their homes with the blessing of the family who remained behind. New families also began among the young women and men who busied themselves in the Lord's work but somehow found time to fall in love. These marriages help explain the close interconnections among some families in the movement even to this day. All in all, it is fair to say that the Church of God movement's early communal practices enlarged the idea of family; after all, every Christian could be called "brother" or "sister."

Sebastian Michels' commitments to a broadened practice of the idea of family ran especially deep. Born in London, Ontario in 1850, the boy Sebastian moved with his parents to northern Michigan in 1859. He left home at 13. Six years later he was converted, and in 1882, through the influence of Joseph C. Fisher,

Michels experienced entire sanctification. He then began a ministerial service which continued until his death in 1926. Serving primarily in northern Indiana and Michigan, Michels must be included among the celebrated "flying messengers". Unlike his colleagues, however, Michels settled down rather quickly, making his permanent home in southwestern Michigan. There his commitments took on tangible expression.

Michels carried a special burden for the people who live at either end of our experience of the family, the young and the old. At Grand Junction he and his wife, Chloe, founded a children's home. Initially this home cared for the children of the flying messengers. Michels thought that these youngsters should not be made to endure the hardships and dangers of travel in the companionship of their evangelist parents, and his home was founded out of this concern. Before long, however, the home's occupants included local orphans. Occasionally as many as sixty children lived there. Years later, the Michels founded and superintended the "Old People's Charitable Home" in South Haven, a ministry they continued for almost twenty-five years.

A few of Michels' ministerial colleagues judged him harshly. In the days when evangelism dominated the shape of the ministry in the Church of God, some people accused Michels of abandoning the rigors of the "flying ministry" in favor of more comfortable and secure work in the homes at Grand Junction and South Haven. Only "hireling" preachers forsook the evangelistic ministry, according to the rhetoric of that era. By staying at home with children and old people, Michels, in the minds of some, was flying his true colors which proved him unworthy of the ministerial calling.

The Michels' homes for children and the elderly probably did reveal the true colors of these deeply dedicated servants. That they merit the label "unworthy" surely displays the prejudices of a narrowly conceived notion of ministry. In any event, even this unfair criticism did not deter Sebastian and Chloe. What drove them on, even in the face of narrow, adverse opinion? Perhaps Sebastian's experience as a homeless adolescent stimulated his deep care for children. Another plausible explanation of their tenacity would be to point to the scriptural admonition to the church that it care for widows and orphans in particular. These are, after all, the members of society who often are without social power or privilege and therefore are special objects of God's love and attention. If the Bible enjoins the church to care for these, then Sebastian and Chloe Michels would follow that injunction. Like nearly all Church of God people, the Michels believed that the Bible is more than a book to be believed; it also is to be practiced.

The matter of practicing or performing the scripture is more than a novel expression. Nicholas Lash explains how interpreting the Bible is first of all a matter of practice, because the scripture is intended to be performed; as the church performs the scripture we interpret it to the world. Lash employs this way of thinking about the Bible to rethink an old problem, the relationship between the church and the critical study of scripture. Along the way he offers a refreshing view of the Bible that, I think, also explains the way the Michels understood the Bible even if they would never have expressed themselves in Lash's terms (1986: 37-46).

Different kinds of texts, says Lash, must be interpreted differently. Poetic and musical texts must be sung to be properly interpreted, but few people would sing an airline or railroad timetable. A Shakespearean play, on the other hand, can be read and critically studied for its meaning. However, only when a company of actors and actresses *performs* the script is the play interpreted in its fullest meaning; the play requires performers for its interpretation. Lash wants to make the point that critical scholarship is not the last word on the meaning of the Bible, because it intends to be performed. That performance is the role of the church. But the church, like a company of Shakespearean actors will offer a better interpretation if informed by the work of scholarship. For our purposes, however, it is enough that we understand Lash's observation that the Bible is interpreted as the church performs or practices it.

It seems to me that Sebastian and Chloe Michels founded their homes for children and the elderly as interpreters, that is to say, performers of the Scriptures. In the truest sense, the Bible is much more than a book to be believed. It is to be performed, and in this performance the truthfulness of Scripture lives again and again. Moreover, no solitary individual can perform the Scriptures; a people is required. We call this people the church. As the church performs the Scriptures we give the world an opportunity to see life under God's grace, forgiveness, and love. It is this vision that prompts the world to observe, "Behold, see how these Christians love one another." The church that displays God's love to fellow believers in a manner visible to the world performs the scriptures and witnesses to a bond of perfectness that transforms sinners into the family of God.

Chapter Two Notes

1. *Heralds of a Brighter Day*, 1955, 138. Persons interested in a fuller treatment of Mrs. Hunter's life should read *Madam President: The Story of Nora Hunter* by Hazel G. Neal and Axchie A. Bolitho, revised by Marie Meyer, 1982.

Politics

Friendliness and Friendship

Collett Varner, at the time pastor of the Park Forest Church of God in Ft. Wayne and an old friend since college days, dropped by my office for a visit. I asked him how the congregation was doing, and in the course of answering my question Rev. Varner made an interesting observation. He said, "We are not a friendly church; we are a church where people make friends." That is an extremely important distinction. Considering its implications is a task well worth our time.

These days it seems that friendliness often is confused with friendship. An example of friendliness might be the smile and "Have a nice day" with which clerks at the supermarket check-out dismiss us from their attention. Such civility and pleasantness is important, and most of us enjoy this friendly benediction. But friendliness cannot substitute for friendship.

True friendship links people in the mutual pursuit of shared goods and ideals. In this sense a friend is more than someone who is "there for you," someone upon whom we can rely. To be sure, faithfulness and empathy are important qualities in a friend, but the highest form of friendship draws people together as they seek a good that is beyond them.

The history of the Church of God movement holds several examples of friendship. I think that D. S. Warner and Joseph Fisher enjoyed such a friendship in the movement's earlier days, as did F. G. Smith and R. L. Berry a few decades later. Nora Hunter, Ocie Perry, Hallie Patterson, and the other early leaders of the Women of the Church of God also were friends who mutually pursued a shared good. John A. Morrison and Russell Olt shared goods that transcended both of them and thus were friends in the truest sense of the term.

The Morrison-Olt friendship began about 1924. Morrison was the principal of a Bible training school in Anderson. Olt was the Dean of Wilmington College near Cincinnati; he also served as the pastor of the Walnut Hills Church of God. Morrison badly wanted to see the Bible school grow into a college. He also knew that he lacked the education to guide the school through a period of extensive academic development, but Russell Olt possessed the education needed by such a guide. Morrison and R. R. Byrum persuaded Olt to leave Wilmington and take up the academic leadership of the tiny Bible school. Olt joined the faculty in 1925. That decision launched a friendship that lasted through the joys and heartache, the victories and defeats of the next thirty-three years.

That Olt and Morrison enjoyed such a friendship is remarkable. In many respects the two men had very little in common, as Morrison himself noted. Morrison grew up in the Ozark backwoods, one of many children in a large household that eventually merged with another family. Olt grew up in Dayton, Ohio, an only child in a prosperous, middle-class family. Morrison's very limited formal education looked quite ragged in comparison with Olt's university training. Olt loved travel; Morrison hated it. At vacation time, Olt often headed for New York City; Morrison took off for his cabin in the Ozarks (1962: 152). How could men so different from one another form such a lasting friendship?

It sometimes is the case that opposites are attracted to one another, although that is truer of magnets than friendships. Perhaps Morrison and Olt's personalities, temperaments, and inclinations complemented one another. In their friendship each of them might have become more than he could have but for the presence of his friend, his alter ego. Beyond that hypothesis there remains this: Olt and Morrison shared a common dedication to the task of developing a true college for the people of the Church of God movement.

They prized education as a good, and they believed that such goods as learning are to be shared widely. Underlying their common commitment to education was their common commitment to follow Jesus as Lord and Master. These common commitments sustained the Morrison-Olt friendship through times of institutional crisis and personal disagreements.

Olt and Morrison did not always see eye to eye. On one occasion, when Morrison did not keep a commitment where Olt believed an obligation existed, the dean's anger and sense of betrayal kept him away from his office and his tongue silent for weeks. Eventually, he and Morrison overcame their differences. True friends seek such reconciliation. When Morrison published his autobiography in 1962, he dedicated it to the memory of his late friend of so many years, Russell Olt.

All of us in the church share one common Lord. In that we share the possibility of true friendship. But such friendships flourish only in our common commitment to that Lord who named himself our friend and in our common commitments to the various goods that derive from that divine friendship. Such friendships, gifts of grace, enable our lives to flourish. When our hearts are enriched by the presence of true friends, we realize that friendliness, although pleasant and harmless enough, is roughly akin to pinning on our chests a yellow smiley-face button.

The Margin and Main Street

The word "margin" means the border or edge. It also means a minimum limit below which existence is undesirable at best and impossible at worst. My paternal great-grandfather homesteaded in north-central North Dakota. Compared to the rich cropland of the Red River Valley a few hundred miles to the east, his was a marginal farm. My grandparents took over that farm and raised twelve children on what they could wrest from its thin soil. Their life was good, but hard. My grandparents and their children lived much of their lives on the margin of prosperity—far from its center.

The first two generations of Church of God people lived on another sort of margin. Unlike my grandfather's, their farms, often in the corn belt, were prosperous. Rather, these people lived on the margins of their society. The majority of them were far removed from the center of their society's power and influence. D. S. Warner's parents were farmers, and his father also had kept a cheap tavern. E. E. Byrum's family farmed. Sarah Smith cooked for her farm family until Warner invited her to join his evangelistic company. Nora Siens Hunter was an orphan. S. O. Susag lost one day-labor job after another and was reduced to buying beer at a nickel a glass in saloons because that purchase allowed him to eat the free lunch that accompanied the beer.

Of course, these examples do not tell the whole story. A few people of more socially prominent position and vocation did come into the movement. S. G. Bryant and George Achor both were physicians, but they were part of a decided minority, and they forsook their medical careers to become full-time gospel workers. By and large, however, early Church of God people occupied a social region quite removed from centers of power, prestige, influence, and wealth. These people often alienated the citizens of the communities where they resided. The people of Moundsville and Anderson did not know what to think of the strange people called the "Saints" who lived on the outskirts of their communities. When the Gospel Trumpet company left Moundsville, West Virginia, the town generally was of the opinion that the company's departure was good riddance. Not many early Church of God people were invited to join a country club.

Few people enjoy life on the margin. A marginalized existence is hard, undesirable, and at times impossible. Ironically, it also can be wonderfully egalitarian. In the days when Vince Lombardi coached the Green Bay Packers all the players, veterans and rookies alike, were "marginalized"; only Lombardi held power. Team veterans did not haze rookies in the rough manner of other NFL teams. One veteran explained this unusually generous behavior toward rookies by saying, "Vince treated us all like dogs."

On the margins, people tend to overlook superficial differences that become more important the nearer one approaches the center of society. The rawness of marginalized existence levels differences. One explanation for the great cooperation between blacks and whites, Americans and immigrant groups, and men and women in ministry in the Church of God movement's early days lies in the marginal existence of its people. They occupied the border of their society, far from the influential people who lived on the other side of the tracks. The attitudes and prejudices that divide people at the center of society often go unnoticed on its margins.

People on the margin fail to be impressed by the achievements or successes of those who live and work nearer the center of social power and influence. Most of the things that matter at the center are not very important at the margin. People at the margin do not control the circumstances of their lives; they entertain few illusions about their ability to master their fortunes. It is perhaps that realization that helps some marginalized people treasure their friends and treat their neighborhoods as places of enduring value. People who treasure friendship in the midst of life on the margin live their lives with a flexibility and adaptability unknown by those who believe they hold the keys to success and control. Maybe the reason the marginalized tend to be unimpressed by those at the center is because the margin dwellers recognize the illusion that holds the "powerful" and "successful" captive.

People like D. S. Warner, Allie Fisher, Sarah Smith, S. O. Susag and many, many others knew themselves to be members of a beloved community. They knew this community to be the church, a church of socially powerless, marginalized people. They experienced most of life's hard reversals and its joys as members of this community and with its fellowship. In the deepest sense, they were nourished in this communion of the saints. As such, the allure of success, prestige and power had little to recommend to them. By and large, people on the margin pay little attention to such things; rarely, if ever, do they honor them.

The rawness of life on the margins must grate on those who live there. Its harshness often spawns the desire to move uptown, to get closer to the center of things, to become respectable, to gain some power to create change. Eventually, the early Christian community came to believe that it would be wonderful if Caesar were to get converted and become a Christian. In time, of course, Caesar did get converted. Great for Caesar, but what was great for Caesar turned out to be not so good for the church. Moving uptown may not be everything it's cracked up to be.

On the Church and Peace

The Persian Gulf War came and went with stunning suddenness. Many Americans were filled with apprehension during the military deployment of the "Desert Shield." The technological wizardry of American weapons amazed much of the world; CNN saw to that. "Desert Storm" turned out to be very, very brief, to the relief of all. The whole episode caused me to reflect historically on some ideas about war and peace that have been part of the life and thought of the Church of God movement.

When I was in college and seminary, as the United States waged its longest war, several of my teachers described the Church of God as a "historic peace church." By this phrase they meant to include the movement among those churches that have opposed participation in war—the Mennonites, the Friends and the Brethren. My teachers based their claim on the strong statements against war that early Church of God people published in the *Gospel Trumpet*.

During the Spanish-American War the *Trumpet* said, "There is no place in the New Testament wherein Christ gave instruction to his followers to take the life of a fellow man. . . . Jesus says, 'If thine enemy hunger; feed him; if he thirst give him drink'—not shoot him" (*G.T.* 1899:4). No other editorial comment on war appeared during the "splendid little war" with Spain. Other comments appeared after the war and we may conclude from these statements that Church of God leaders opposed participation in war because (a) war violates Jesus' command to love one's enemies; and (b) the experience of entire sanctification enables men and women to keep this commandment. Nevertheless, (c) Christians are to be good citizens and respect the authority of the state.

Through the medium of the *Trumpet*, E. E. Byrum and F. G. Smith both opposed Christians' participation in war. Byrum's convictions may have been shaped by his religious background in the River Brethren, a group with historic and doctrinal connections to the peace churches of the Radical Reformation. Smith, on the other hand, seems to have based his opposition to war on a holiness position: sanctified Christians do not sin; killing is sin; therefore, Christians do not kill. Smith's convictions on this matter led him to help organize a peace fellowship in the Church of God movement.

As I say, this position against Christian involvement in war was taught through the pages of the *Gospel Trumpet*. But sufficient evidence exists to suggest that by the end of World War I the movement's practice of pacifism lagged behind its preaching. Although the *Trumpet* ran articles advising young men on how to apply for status or, if necessary, enter military service as conscientious objectors, some of the movement's men fought in the Great War, ironically, *on both sides*. Only God knows whether there was a tragic moment when people of the Church of God actually were shooting at one another in World War I; it could have happened. Although the *Trumpet* restated the movement's convictions against the taking of human life, it also stated that no man should be "Un-Christianized" for going into battle.

How might we account for the difference between preaching and practice on the war issue in the Church of God? A great host of possibilities suggest themselves. Maybe the preachers were not really convinced of the truth of their opposition to war. Maybe they were not effective in their teaching. Maybe the loose-knittedness of the movement and its antiorganizational biases inhibited effective church discipline. Maybe the young men who went off to war found the call of patriotism irresistible. Maybe they felt obligated to defend their "neighbor," i.e. the weak and defenseless. Each of these reasons, or some combination of them, might explain the difference between our words and our deeds. Some reasons are more plausible than others. Some are theologically more convincing than others: we ought to take very seriously the idea that one may go to war to defend those who are incapable of defending themselves.

Although many men of the Church of God did follow the teaching on war, I think that in general the movement has ignored its own theological opposition to war. The reason we have not practiced all that we preached lies not so much in the possibilities listed above as in the movement's failure to limit the government's claims on our lives. As the United States grew ever more involved in World War I, the tone of *Gospel Trumpet* comment changed. The paper stopped short of endorsing the war, but it also stated that Americans have a duty to their country. To grant the state sufficient authority to require or even expect Christians to kill undermines the church's position against war. Sooner or later, Caesar will insist on his pinch of incense.

Christians are people of the resurrection before they are citizens of a state even as free and generous as the American. As James McLendon ably argues, Jesus' resurrection has implications for our lives beyond hope and comfort in the face of death. The resurrection is that, to be sure, but it is much more. The resurrection has moral implications for our lives as well. As people of the resurrection we learn to construe the world from the point of view of the resurrected Lord who taught us about a present kingdom over which God reigns. Where God reigns, Caesar may not have the first place—and Caesars of any time and place cannot abide being second fiddle.

Advent of 1990 was a season of uneasiness. Some of my former students were deployed in Saudi Arabia, as were friends and children of many Church of God people. The nation had resolved not to forsake the forces of Desert Shield as the Vietnam veterans had been forsaken. Soldiers were doing their duty as is the soldier's lot.

Who keeps Caesar in his place? Who but the church in America can remind Caesar that his claims cannot be ultimate? Who but the church can see the world from the perspective of the resurrection?

Worldly Entertainment

I still remember the day when I came home from Newport Elementary School with the news that our teacher had promised to show us and the other class of third-graders how to square-dance. The cold reception that my mother gave this announcement only introduced me to a list of prohibited activities the length of which I had not yet begun to fathom. I was about to learn that several forms of entertainment enjoyed by my friends at school were forbidden to me. Church of God people who can remember back twenty years or more can readily list several of these activities: dancing, movies, playing pool ("right here in River City"); card-playing (except for Rook). Go back another generation and the list lengthens to include bowling, reading novels, attending parties and fairs, and games where both sexes simultaneously participated. Women and men could play volleyball and croquet on the lawn of the Trumpet Home in Anderson—but not in mixed company.

The origins of this essentially negative attitude toward "worldly amusements" can be partially located deep in the American past. Nineteenth century American Protestants believed in and practiced what historians have come to call the "Puritan Sabbath." H. L. Mencken once described Puritanism as "the sneaking suspicion that somewhere somebody was having a good time." Although Mencken caricatured the Puritans as drab killjoys, it is nevertheless the case that they took a strict and serious attitude toward life. It was preparation for eternity and no laughing matter. Some of the Puritan attitude carried over into the nineteenth century. It reinforced Protestant suspicions of the city as a place of idleness and mischief. Part of the Puritan ethic also included the notion that people live in order to work. This attitude lent great dignity to the idea of work and simultaneously stigmatized the idea of play. Like other American Protestants, early Church of God preachers and teachers were heirs to these traditions, and they readily found their way into the movement's theological and moral life.

Two additional reasons must be put forward to help us understand the baleful glance that the Church of God movement has cast toward worldly entertainments. Both of these reasons have to do with our attitude toward that which we have termed "the world." First: the Church of God historically has understood the world to be a dangerous place. The Saints might be tempted by the seductions of the world—that which was outside of and hostile to the reign of God. Even sincere Christians might lose their way among all the seductive blandishments that the world offered. The world, in this sense, was to be feared—and earnest Christians would stay as far away from "the world" as possible. No good could come to the life of the person who made a habit of trafficking there.

Related to our suspicion of the world is a second reason for our prohibition on certain worldly amusements. I protested my mother's announcement that I would not be square-dancing with the rest of that wanton group of third-graders by asking the question that hundreds, perhaps thousands, of others before and after me have asked—"WHY?" The reason was simple, or so I was told. We were different. Not necessarily better than the Schottmullers, good Methodists who lived just down Second Avenue from us, but different. In a real sense we were to understand that our commitment to Jesus marked us. The shunning of certain worldly amusements served as one of those marks. We did not prohibit forms of entertainment simply to be different, but as a consequence of our discipleship.

As I reflect on this aspect of our history, let us keep a few ideas in view. I think, for example, that it is a mistake to cast off our forefathers' and foremothers' concerns about entertainment as quaint or odd relics from a rural Protestant past. While early Church of God people may have been mistaken about some specific forms of amusement, on balance one must regard their suspicion of the world as a good thing. Money, sex, and power are preoccupations of the world and the contemporary entertainment industry that serves it. All three are also among the world's most powerful and seductive temptations—which is a good reason why Christians have been worrying about them for nearly two thousand years.

Second, the matter of entertainment is itself highly problematic, especially in the age of television. The question of entertainment and Christians is larger than simply asking what forms of amusement are appropriate for Christians. In an alarming book titled *Amusing Ourselves to Death*, Neil Postman examines television's great power as a medium of entertainment. He goes on to observe that this power is so great as to transform all forms of televised public discourse (news programs, education, religious worship) into entertainment. As it does this, television trains us to demand that we be entertained by the live forms of public discourse in which we participate. This expectation in the life of the church is entertainment run amok, for insofar as we come to church to watch and listen rather than to participate in worship, we make ourselves and our desire for entertainment the center of "worship." Is there a worse form of idolatry than one that substitutes us for God as the object of worship?

Finally, it remains important to ask ourselves how we are different from the world in which we live. The world God created nevertheless remains a dangerous place. The church nevertheless is called to live in this world as the people of God. We are "resident aliens" as Stanley Hauerwas and William Willimon have observed in their provocative book of that title (1989). Our calling is not to be different, so that we will simply look for signs by which to mark ourselves off from the world. Rather, we are called to be faithful to God and in God's power and grace be conformed to God. Such conformation will touch all aspects of our lives, including money, sex, power, leisure, and entertainment—and the false notion that we have these as rights, as something to which we are entitled. Such conformation will undoubtedly cause us to be regarded as odd people by a world that sees these matters quite differently.

The Bodies Politic

The marriage between political campaigning and television is so healthy that their divorce seems quite unlikely, however desirable it might be. In 1960 political advisers were only beginning to discover the power of television in shaping an election campaign. I remember early "paid political advertisements" for both presidential candidates, Richard Nixon and John Kennedy. I recall with far greater clarity my three-year-old brother's response whenever Senator Kennedy's image appeared on the screen. "Kennedy," he would say, "Yuck!" My brother did not base his disapproval on the fact that we were Republicans. Actually, my parents were independent voters. The source of this toddler's anti-Kennedy politics lay more in the fact that we were Church of God and Kennedy was Catholic.

Editorials about the "religion question" of the presidential campaign began appearing in the *Gospel Trumpet* in February 1960. By then the question of Kennedy's religious affiliation had been thoroughly discussed in a variety of public forums. Should a candidate's personal religious preference be a political consideration? Is it a matter for the voters to consider? The force of the *Trumpet* editorial clearly answered these questions in the affirmative. Voters possess "the right to decide to what extent [they] think a given candidate is in fact unfettered and to what extent a candidate might be dictated to by particular pressure groups, be they political or religious, or a combination of the two" (*G.T.* Feb 14, 1960: 3).

The issue of Kennedy's religion frequently returned to the pages of the *Trumpet* throughout 1960. Sometimes the paper reported material taken from the Religious News Service. Allegedly reporting news rather than offering editorial opinion, these articles nevertheless tended to reinforce the point of view taken in the quotation cited earlier. Without endorsing Nixon, they discussed the religion question in a manner that implied that Kennedy could not be supported. On the basis of its own editorials, the *Gospel Trumpet* would have to be said to have opposed the election of John Kennedy on the grounds of his Catholicism.

Trumpet readers also expressed their views on both the campaign and the paper's editorial stance. The majority warned that Kennedy's candidacy jeopardized American freedoms. Something had to be done to save the country from the imminent danger of papal domination. But at least one letter writer objected to the *Trumpet's* editorial "insinuations," calling them "obnoxious" (*G.T.* Oct. 23, 1960: 16).

From the privileged vantage point of 1990 the printed opinions of 1960 seem quaintly innocent, if not naive. In that year comment on the Kennedy-Nixon campaign suggests that people of the Church of God did not dream that religion could be used as a tool to gain votes. We have since learned that personal faith has meant much to some of our presidents and virtually nothing to others despite their public statements. Jimmy Carter taught a Baptist Sunday school class. Yet Ronald Reagan defeated Carter with the help of evangelical Christians. Mr. Reagan's wife, it will be remembered, consulted astrologers to help this evangelical champion plan his day. Maybe we are no longer so naive.

Another of the lessons of the last thirty years may be that we are beginning to realize that politics and religion are not so easily separated as we once thought. In point of fact, the only way to separate them is to make politics the public aspect of human life and consign religion to the inner, private, and individual. This is a serious mistake for both religious and political life.

The problem with such a separation is that it is false to the notion of religion that the Church of God movement has generally understood. One cannot be a Christian, we have said, without going public. To be a child of God is to "let a holy life tell the gospel story." The life of discipleship necessarily leads to life in the public arena. Once we have gone public and the religious nature of our commitments has been disclosed, we will find religion and politics mixed together in a variety of ways. This ought to be the case. The challenge, is to form our political commitments out of the gospel story rather than according to the agenda of party politics.

What's In a Name?

The first people in the Church of God movement to use the term "flying messengers" meant by it the pace of their own travel and their essential homelessness. "Flying messengers" signified a people on the move. Even the Gospel Trumpet Company was on the move—literally—in those days.

Between 1880 and 1886 the *Trumpet* was published at Rome City, Indiana; Indianapolis; Cardington and Bucyrus in Ohio; and Williamston, Michigan. The *Trumpet* family called Grand Junction, Michigan home for roughly twelve years. Then, the same year that Teddy Roosevelt and the Rough Riders charged up San Juan Hill, the company hired a train to relocate in Moundsville, West Virginia. The business-minded Byrums, Editor E. E. and Treasurer N. H., saw the wisdom of fueling the company's steam engines on West Virginia coal bought for as little as thirty-five cents per ton. At Grand Junction they had paid three dollars. One move remained for this peripatetic company; in 1906 they journeyed to Anderson.

Neither the flying messengers or the Gospel Trumpet Company became very attached to *places*. That much seems evident from what we have just recounted. Neither did it occur to them to identify the Church of God movement by reference to a particular place. Today we commonly refer to ourselves as the "Church of God (Anderson, Indiana)." A place has become the way in which we often distinguish ourselves from others who carry the same name or another that resembles it. Why have we chosen to identify ourselves by reference to a geographical location, especially when so much of our early history reads like the Book of Numbers?

Groups need means of identification. Even a movement committed to Christian unity will eventually develop means for discerning insiders and outsiders. But places need not be the means by which these important distinctions are made. We could distinguish ourselves from others on the basis of ideas or virtues that convey the essence of who we are. In the era of the flying messengers we used words like "anti-sectarian," "holiness," and "radical" to describe the message that was the very core of our being. How might we be different today had we continued to define ourselves by ideas rather than a place?

I wonder if some of the movement's early dynamism, its pilgrim orientation, slipped away when we took the admittedly logical step of referring to ourselves through the place where the general offices were located. Is identification by geography accompanied by settledness, a comfortableness in which the ferment of God's presence has a difficult time bubbling through? Remember that all of us, regardless of where we live, are inclined now to think of the movement as the "Church of God (Anderson, Indiana)."

Perhaps I am fretting about matters that cannot be changed. Maybe humans simply must put down roots in places. But Christians do that at some cost to their self-understanding and sense of mission. So these words, spoken about Christians of an era long gone, remind us of the possibility of being Christians anywhere; for us no place and every place is home.

> They dwell in their own countries, but only as sojourners; they bear their share in all things as citizens, and they endure all hardships as strangers. Every foreign country is a fatherland to them, and every fatherland is foreign....Their existence is on earth, but their citizenship is in heaven. They obey the established laws, and they surpass the laws in their own lives. They love all men, and they are persecuted by all. They are ignored, and yet they are condemned. They are put to death, and yet they are endued with life. They are in beggary, and yet they make many rich (Lightfoot 1956: 254).

Situational Christianity

D. S. Warner positively despised the attempts, which he saw all around him, to organize God's church. The General Eldership of the Churches of God withdrew Warner's ministerial credentials. Another religious organization, the Indiana State Holiness Association, rejected Warner's amendment to its bylaws article on membership. The association required all of its members to hold membership in a "recognized denomination," and it refused Warner's modification of that 'sect endorsing clause,' as he described it. In rejecting Warner's amendment the association rejected him. Thus on two separate occasions D. S. Warner felt himself to be oppressed by the weight of ecclesiastical machinery. Small wonder that he hated organization, whether of the church or in it. We should not be surprised that he reserved some of his sharpest epithets for church organizations and their supporters.

Warner's deep misgivings about organization bequeathed to the Church of God movement a long-term suspicion of organized religion. Nevertheless, after Warner's death the movement began taking small steps toward organization. For example, we began the practice of voting. Warner had considered the casting of ballots an unscriptural, Babylonian act.

One of Warner's successors as *Trumpet* Editor, Charles E. Brown, said that the Church of God movement had organized neither religion nor church. Rather, he said, we organized the *work* of the church. This neat separation eased the consciences of some of the saints who had been troubled by the rapid growth in the number and size of the movement's "agencies" during the period 1917 to 1930. To these tender souls the organizational growth of those years looked to be the very sort of "ecclesiasticism" which Warner had condemned.

Brown's notion of organizing the church's work but not the church itself calmed the fears of many, and the movement has allowed Brown's distinction between the church and its work to justify our organizations, whether at local, state, or national levels. But does anyone possess a knife sharp enough to separate the church and its work?

Could it be the case that Brown's distinction between the church and its work allowed us to overlook deeper problems in the very nature of organized religion, whether the church or its work? For example, the essayist Wendell Berry thinks that Christianity organized either as the church or its work is highly problematic. "The *organized* church," he says, "comes immediately under a compulsion to think of itself and identify itself to the world, not as an institution synonymous with its truth and its membership, but as a hodgepodge of funds, properties, projects and offices, all urgently requiring economic support" (1990: 95-96). Organizing the church's work as such, Berry continues, "requires the church to be dependent on 'the economy.' " But we daily witness the destructiveness of this economy. Our society struggles under the enormous waste—the bad stewardship—of an economy that exploits people and the creation rather than nurturing them. So we have this irony: "the organized church cannot survive apart from those economic practices that its truth forbids, that its vocation is to correct" (96). Berry touches an important nerve. His contention certainly merits our serious consideration. I mention it here because he has set me to wondering again about D. S. Warner's deep misgivings concerning the organization of the church and about Brown's separation of church and work. Do we need to re-think our understanding of the organized work of the church? If Berry is correct, then organizing the church's work is as problematic as organizing the church. At least that would seem to be the case if we draw our organizational models from an economy that destroys rather than practices good stewardship.

Richard John Neuhaus describes sectarianism as "reinventing Christianity to suit the circumstances," and then in a fine phrase he terms this "situational Christianity" (1987: 3). The church, in organizing its work, would seem to adapt itself to an economy that utterly disregards the creation that God termed good. That adaptation is sectarian in an excessively spiritual way. Berry points out the self-contradiction of this spiritual and economic sectarianism: "If one is living by the tithes of history's most destructive economy, then the disembodiment of the soul becomes the chief of worldly conveniences" (Berry, 1990: 96).

If Berry and Neuhaus are correct, then D. S. Warner was more right to fear organization in the church than even he knew. By the same token, C. E. Brown prematurely ended the conversation about organization that Warner had begun and which the movement should by all lights continue. By ending that conversation, Brown enabled us to organize the church's "work" with a clear conscience—maybe too clear and too easy.

Shared Responsibility

By default, the office of Historian entitles its holder to the attention and gifts of people who have a historical interest in the Church of God movement. So it was that Harold Phillips, former Editor in

Chief at Warner Press, once gave me an unusual gift of real historical importance. It is a slender volume of the Gospel Trumpet
Company *Workers' Bulletin*, all twelve monthly issues for the year
1911. Each month the company published a detailed list of the
names and responsibilities of every person who was a member of
the Trumpet Family. This small bulletin, only four pages in length,
lists workers according to the company's division of labor and
identifies the state or country that each worker left to come to
Anderson. Because the Trumpet home in Anderson also housed the
missionary activities of the flying messengers, people constantly
arrived from evangelistic tours and departed for further service.
The *Trumpet Workers' Bulletin* faithfully reported the names of
travelers coming to and leaving the home. Some men and women
joined the Trumpet family only for a brief season. Circumstances
forced other long-term workers to return to the homes they had left
to join the Trumpet work. All of these arrivals and departures were
duly noted in the *Bulletin*.

To read through the 1911 volume of the *Trumpet Workers'
Bulletin* is to enter into the well-ordered and yet relentlessly active
world of the Gospel Trumpet family. Although they may have lived
together in the Trumpet home as a family, as the movement's publishing house the members of the company were also organized
into well-defined divisions of labor. Some of these divisions are
obvious: office, sales, purchasing, correspondence, editorial, manu-
facturing, and printing. No doubt many of the young men and
women who felt called to join the Trumpet work arrived in town
believing that they would be assigned to one such division. After
all, they had left home to join in the great work of publishing the
message of the Church of God movement. In 1911, however, the
Gospel Trumpet Company still lived together, for the most part, as
a communal society. That fact required some family members to be
assigned work that was apparently only remotely connected to the
publication and distribution of Christian literature.

Along with company divisions assigned the responsibility for
production and distribution, others were organized for the support
of the entire company. The Trumpet Home division was thus subdi-
vided into departments where Trumpet workers were assigned to
jobs in the kitchen or laundry, the sewing room or storehouse, or as

Not all members of the Gospel Trumpet Company were directly involved with the publication and distribution of religious literature. Organized as a communal society until 1917, the Trumpet Company required the support services of many individuals. Pictured here are company bookkeepers, cooks, and firefighters.

janitors or watchmen. The company's organization overlooked no detail needed for the support of workers dedicated to the publishing work. The company's Trumpet home division even had a barber and watch repairer, and a department called "Department of Chamber Work and Extra Help."

Other members of the Trumpet Company worked in its Outside Work Division. In 1911 Arnold Zach and G. L. Welling did the blacksmithing in this division of the company's labor. Emery Stephens ran the dairy, and M. L. Roseberry repaired the Trumpet family's shoes. J. W. Talley cared for the animals stabled in the company's barn, and W. D. Garman tended the garden that produced many of the fruits and vegetables destined for the Trumpet family's common table. Mary Wiland and J. H. Stanley took care of the Trumpet chickens. One wonders whether these men and women came to Anderson intending to do such work. Did they have any inkling that their call to gospel service would carry them to a chicken coop, a cobbler's bench, or a stable?

The number of people working in the Gospel Trumpet Company varied rather widely across the year 1911. The July bulletin reported 247 workers in the company, the low figure for that year. The peak number of company workers was 294 in November. No explanation of this rather broad fluctuation is offered, and without such explanation we are left to wonder how production and distribution supervisors coped with the problems created by a semitransient work force. Following is an excerpt from the January report of arrivals and departures:

> Since the 11th we have been favored with the presence of Amos and Edith Abernethy and two small children. They had just recently returned from India.
>
> Sister E. Faith Stewart arrived on the 18th and remained about two weeks before continuing her journey eastward.
>
> From the 4th to the 11th Frances B. Tallen enjoyed a visit at Maude Smith's home at Mentone, Ind. Sister Brookover [the home matron] and Zella, who were also there, returned on the 4th.
>
> Fred Vance assisted in the work from the 10th to the 30th, when he returned to Iowa.

> After several years' faithful labor in the bindery, Sister Marian Rodger has gone to Chicago to help in the Missionary Home there.
>
> J. Frank Shaw, who has been steward for some time, has gone to Martins Ferry, Ohio, where he will help Brother and Sister Dodge in the gospel work (*Worker's Bulletin*, 1911, n. p.).

The simple, almost laconic entries of the 1911 *Workers' Bulletin* portray a large group of men and women bound together by a shared vocation. "Vocation" here must be understood in its original sense of "calling." Aspiring Trumpet workers were not "job seekers." Rather, they traveled to Anderson from throughout the United States and beyond in answer to a call to join in a great work. When they arrived at the Trumpet offices and received their working assignments, it may have been that notion of vocation that kept them at such homely tasks as laundering clothes or tending chickens. A vision of the larger enterprise that their service sustained surely gave purpose to Trumpet workers who could just as well have milked cows or cared for horses back home.

The Gospel Trumpet Home served as a model for dozens of missionary homes that were founded in the early days of the movement's history. The manner in which the Trumpet workers shared responsibility for the publishing work also exemplifies the church at it best. The church is not a place where managers lead and the remainder of the people simply follow like sheep. The church is a body, an interrelated whole wherein each member shares in the responsibility and mission of the entire organism. In this body all have their appointed work, and the work of each member is essential to the health of the entire body. No assignment is insignificant; no worker is of greater value than another. Every person's work contributes to the health and faithfulness of the congregation as a whole. From the glimpse of Trumpet company life revealed to us in the *Trumpet Workers' Bulletin*, then, we might draw a picture of the church as an interrelated organism where responsibility is shared, where each person is valued, and where everyone has an assignment to fill.

Agencies and Authority

The earliest foreign missionaries of the Church of God left the United States before 1900. No missionary board recruited or sent them. They did not come together for a great, candlelit commissioning ceremony. These early missionaries simply felt called of God, and they went. They spent their lives and resources until they were exhausted. Some of these missionaries would return home, seeking new resources for their work. Others remained on the field and sent home urgent requests for assistance.

In 1897 Gorham Tufts traveled to India carrying funds intended for famine relief and the support of converts already at work there. Money for missions had been mailed to the Gospel Trumpet Company. No other legal entity of the Church of God existed, so the publishing house assumed responsibility for the receipt and disbursement of missions funds. The *Gospel Trumpet* made appeals for money, and its editor, E. E. Byrum, distributed it as he saw fit.

The ministers assembled for the 1909 Anderson Camp Meeting took a momentous step in support of a more systematized missionary effort. At that meeting plans were put forward for the publication of a missions paper, *Missionary Herald*, and the constitution of a seven member missionary board composed of people capable of "advising, instructing, encouraging and restraining" (Tasker 1981: 37). The board's existence gave tangible evidence of the movement's commitment to missionary work, but the creation of a board also stepped across the movement's barrier against organizations in the church. The ministers who stood and voiced their "amen" to the proposal for a missionary board created a precedent that led to the establishment of other boards and agencies during the next two decades. As in the case of the missionary board, these new agencies came into being to advise and assist work already in progress; home missionaries were at work before the creation of the Board of Church Extension and Home Missions, just as we had Sunday schools before the Board of Christian Education. The agencies were created to assist the church rather than to tell it what to do. Still, many saints were skeptical of these new developments.

C. E. Brown, the fourth editor of the Gospel Trumpet Company, thought that the early leaders' bias against organization was one of our most serious theological and political errors. As he put the matter, "There can be very little cooperation among people who regard all organization as sin" (1954: 112). Brown believed that cooperation was essential to the accomplishment of the church's work; where there is little cooperation, little is accomplished. One of Brown's achievements as editor was to help the movement understand and accept the usefulness and necessity of the numerous agencies that had popped up during the decade just before he came into office. Yet even today the status of our national agencies is anomalous for some in the movement and downright problematic for others.

The four words used to describe the role of the first missionary board illustrate the problem. Board members were to be capable of "advising, instructing, encouraging and restraining." The last word in the sequence implies an executive authority not possessed by any of its three predecessors. Advice can be rejected. Teachers know that they do not always have the full attention of their students. Encouragement is not always well-received or received at all. But when something—or someone—is *restrained*, that's another matter. The capability of restraining connotes a kind of power out of keeping with the spirit of advice, instruction, and encouragement. I think it is also out of keeping with a church tradition that takes for its example one who washed his disciples' feet.

Authority and organization surely are necessary if the church is to get on with its witness in the world. Having said that, however, we have still left open the questions of the kind of authority and organization needful in the church. Attempts to answer those questions will be served better by reference to the power and authority displayed in Jesus' life and ministry than to an executive mentality that thinks its job is to be in charge. The latter conception of authority was the target of the animus toward organization so clearly demonstrated by the movement's early saints: "to man-rule [we] will not bow." In Jesus' life, however, authority was not so much a matter of being in charge as it was the capacity for helping others fulfill the work God had for them to do, even as Jesus had come not to do his own will, but the will of the one who had sent him.

New Wine and Old Skins

During 1992 no fewer than four institutions of the Church of God movement celebrated their diamond anniversaries. In this one year the General Assembly, the National Association of the Church of God, the National Association's General Assembly, and Anderson University all turned seventy-five years of age. Clearly, strong winds of change must have been blowing back in 1917. In that same year both the Missionary Board and the Gospel Trumpet Company also were reorganized as agencies of the General [Ministerial] Assembly, and the Trumpet Company abandoned the communal life-style in which it had been organized ever since its beginning in 1880.

Even the *Yearbook of the Church of God* underwent a wholesale revamping in 1917, becoming a true yearbook for the movement rather than a simple list of ministers. By most reckonings, then, 1917 must be considered a watershed in the life of the Church of God movement. Changes of sweeping proportion which forever altered the movement's way of living together crowded into that single year. Several questions arise whenever such extensive change occurs so rapidly. We should ask ourselves why all these organizations were created within such a brief time span. What forces might have caused these changes? What characteristics did Church of God people possess in 1917 that enabled or permitted them to consider and ultimately adopt such massive changes in the way the movement organized its work? Before considering these questions, perhaps we ought to review the scope of organizational change in 1917 and gain a fresh sense of the difference it made in the movement.

The first *Yearbook* appeared in 1917, and it clearly represented a deviation from previous ministerial lists. Indeed, J. W. Phelps, Registrar and the person responsible for assembling the information recorded in the *Yearbook*, noted this change for its users. The movement had published ministerial lists for the sake of people outside the church—the officials of the Railway Clergy Bureaus who used such lists to authorize reduced fares for ministers traveling as passengers on the trains. On the other hand the *Yearbook*, said Phelps, was published for the sake of the church; it was

intended as a means of information to keep "the different congregations working in harmony so that their efforts will be directed
toward a common end in such a way that the efforts put forth will
bring the greatest results" (1917: 3). The movement had grown to
such size and scope that information about its ministers and congregations was necessary. The *Yearbook* served as the principal
means by which this information was available. Phelps thought that
increased levels of information would improve the quality and
availability of ministry in the movement. Thus the *Yearbook* was
not intended as a statistical source, but as a means of edifying the
church. Phelps was sensitive to the possibility that some would
regard the enlarged *Yearbook* as a threat to the spiritual nature of
the church, but he also believed that the movement's growing numbers and geographical expansion required new measures.

At the same moment when some in the movement had begun
thinking about the church and its ministry in new ways, the very
nature of conversations among the clergy were also being formalized and thus changed from their former character. Ministerial
assemblies were a common feature of nearly every camp meeting
or revival. These meetings were quite informal, however, often
amounting to a gathering of preachers in some semiprivate location
of the campground. No agenda ordered these conversations, since
they were entirely *ad hoc* in nature. Participants kept no written
accounts or summaries. Ministers discussed theological matters,
the general state of the church, or whatever other matters they
deemed important. Although such meetings convened regularly in
conjunction with the general camp meeting in Anderson after 1906,
it was not until 1917 that they were organized as the General
Ministerial Assembly.

In 1917 the leadership of the Gospel Trumpet Company came to
the Anderson assembly with a slate of candidates for membership
in the company. The company asked the ministers gathered in the
assembly to elect these individuals to office, thereby establishing a
precedent and apparently creating one of the precipitating causes
for the formalization of the General Ministerial Assembly. During
that same camp meeting motions were ordered for a temporary
organization to conduct business [very little existed in a movement
that frowned on organization] and the creation of a committee to

draft bylaws. E. A. Reardon was elected chairman *pro tem*, and appointed to the bylaws committee were J. W. Phelps, A. B. Frost, H. A. Sherwood, O. E. Line, and R. R. Byrum. This committee accomplished its work within the term of that same camp meeting, for on June 21, 1917 its report was approved and the General Ministerial Assembly duly constituted.[1]

The Assembly's establishment altered the status of two entities already in existence. The Gospel Trumpet Company was, of course, much older than the assembly and, in a sense, older than the movement itself. The Home and Foreign Missionary Board, created in 1909, also antedated the assembly. The formalization of the ministerial assembly created an organizational logic by which it seemed appropriate that these two entities be regarded as agencies of the assembly. That the Gospel Trumpet Company had presented its slate of nominees to the assembly for election only served to strengthen the force of this logic. Thus the creation of the General Assembly signified the reorganization of the publishing house and the missionary board.

The General Ministerial Assembly which convened during the camp meeting at Anderson was but one of two General Assemblies created in 1917. At the insistence of Elijah P. Wimbish, the National Association of the Church of God created its own General Ministerial Assembly in that same year. Indeed, the National Association itself also was founded in 1917. Unlike the founding of the Anderson assembly, however, the National Association and its assembly came into being at least partly through the movement's tacit acceptance of the racial barriers that deeply divided American society in the first half of the twentieth century.

In the late 1800s and early 1900s, African-Americans began migrating from the American south to the large industrial cities of the north. This broad social movement had a direct bearing on the Church of God movement. Blacks had embraced the movement's message of Christian unity, and some evidence exists to suggest that blacks and whites maintained close relationships in the movement's early days. The social pressure of racism deteriorated these relationships so that by 1916 formerly interracial congregations in the north were dividing along the same color line that ran through American society. In 1917 this division reached the national level, when it was decided that, "for evangelistic reasons" a separate camp meeting for African-Americans was desirable. Wimbish and other black leaders picked up on this hint, and the National Association and its camp meeting at West Middlesex, Pennsylvania, were inaugurated that same year. R. J. Smith, himself a leader of the Pittsburgh missionary home, took office as the first chair of the Association's Assembly.[2]

The development of the National Association and its agencies presents a new and ambiguous dimension to the changes occurring in the movement. On one hand, the creation of associations and agencies by and for African-Americans created many more opportunities for leadership development than had been the case prior to this quasi-separation. On the other hand, to divide the body of Christ for any reason threatened to undermine the movement's message of Christian unity in the presence of the sanctifying Spirit.

Along with its subordinate relationship to the newly created General Assembly, the Gospel Trumpet Company changed in another important respect in 1917. Until that year it had been organized after the fashion of a religious commune. These were the years of the celebrated "Trumpet home" which became something of a model for approximately forty-five missionary homes across the United States. The Trumpet home exceeded all the others in the extent of its communal living arrangements. Workers at the Gospel Trumpet Company received no salaries for their work, but lived together in the company home, took their meals in common, and wore clothing made and provided by the company. In its early years the company was small enough that this communal life style posed few practical problems. But by 1917 the group had grown to such a size and complexity that communal living arrangements were nearly impossible. Younger workers, for example, married and had children who eventually filled the halls of the Trumpet home with many sounds that bore not even the slightest resemblance to the melodies of Zion. Older workers found themselves living in a very different society than the one to which they originally had been called. Such developments forced the company to abandon its communal life style in 1917. This decision left vacant the building that had housed the Trumpet family. An enterprising Texan named J. T. Wilson had an idea for that building's use.

Wilson thought that the vacant Trumpet home would make an ideal location for a Bible training school for ministers and gospel workers. From 1910 to 1920 no fewer than four Bible training schools were founded, each of them connected in some fashion with a missionary home: Spokane, Kansas City, New York, and Anderson. While Wilson's idea thus was not exactly new, the Bible school at Anderson did benefit from a central location to and from which a great deal of the movement's activities flowed. The school also benefited from Wilson's boundless enthusiasm and vision for it. Over the next several years, these two factors contributed strongly to the growth of Anderson Bible Training School. Eventually it overshadowed the other training schools.

The Anderson school's development did not occur without opposition. Many of the movement's leaders opposed the idea that men and women could be prepared for the ministry through formal education. Although D. S. Warner had considered the idea of a ministerial training school shortly before his death in 1895, neither E. E. Byrum nor F. G. Smith, his successors as editor of *The Gospel Trumpet*, used that influential position to support the founding of any of the Bible institutes created during the period from 1910-1920. In fact, both men opposed the idea of schools. J. T. Wilson was not the sort of man to back down from a fight, however, so he looked for people who were willing to lead the infant school through what promised to be a difficult childhood and adolescence. John A. Morrison and Russell Olt took up the positions of president and dean of the embryonic college and guided it through its most difficult decades of growth. The movement's struggle over questions related to formal education came to a head from 1929 to 1934, and this struggle became one of the paradigmatic events of the entire movement.[3]

The winds of change blew heavily through the Church of God movement in 1917 and the years immediately preceding and succeeding it. For many in the movement the real question was whether all this change was the result of the fresh breeze of the Holy Spirit or the hot,wind of apostasy. Were these new opportunities innovative forms of ministry or compromise with the world?

One way to interpret all these developments is to remember that both the Church of God movement and the American society in which it existed were becoming increasingly complex. The movement's growing size and geographical spread presented it with problems that required new solutions. These took the form of what sociologists call institutionalization. The movement's growing internal size and complexity created a kind of internal pressure to develop new institutions, forms of organization, to meet the challenges of the new situation. It also is the case that American society was becoming increasingly complex. Thus the society itself exerted an external pressure on the movement to develop institutions that would enable it to deal with the society in which the movement found itself.

Some will suspect this angle of vision on these events. After all, as I often tell my students, that which sociologists call "socialization and institutionalization" Church of God preachers often have called "compromise with the world"; the former sounds far less threatening than the latter. I must confess my own distrust of institutions, for they often corrupt the very practices they are intended to sustain, but lately I have been reminded that we are not islands unto ourselves. We live through institutions, as it were. They are not in themselves reasons for their own existence, which is to say that neither the General Assembly nor Anderson University nor any of the movement's other agencies created in 1917 (or any other year) exists for itself or to give its officers something to do. Rather such institutions help us to live in social arrangements that sustain the practices that are the real joy and meaning of our life together. The change that blew through the movement in 1917, therefore, must be seen as our effort to create institutions through which men and women might live as followers of Jesus and better love a world full of sin and alienation, which God nevertheless loves.

A Flip-Flop on Tithing

December brings with it Christmas and the Christ's Birthday Observance. Those of us born after World War II can scarcely remember Christmas in the Church of God movement without also thinking of this annual offering. Offerings have been part of the Church of God way from the beginning, but gifts did not always come in the form of money. Early offerings to the Trumpet Home might be a case of home canned meat, cartons of dried fruit, some bushels of vegetables, or the like. Offerings sometimes consisted of old clothing. S. O. Susag, an evangelist active during the first half of this century, once received a heavy coat—just the kind he needed to keep out the harsh winters of the upper Midwest and Canadian prairie provinces.

These offerings in kind should not come as any great surprise to us. The Church of God movement began among people who lived close to the soil. If farming was not their own livelihood, it likely had been that of their parents. Moreover, cash was a controversial subject in the early days of the movement. In 1896 William Jennings Bryan had electrified Democrats at their convention in Chicago with his "Cross of Gold" speech. Farmers and laborers were for "free silver" and a readier cash supply than gold-oriented, banking interests.

Small wonder that about 1900 Church of God people opposed tithing. They gave to the Lord's work, but they did not tithe. J. C. Blaney, a pioneer evangelist to Canada, suggested that congregations follow Jesus' own practice of using a treasury box. As his disciples gathered offerings "for the needs of the work and the poor," so the people of the New Testament church in 1903 ought to be given a chance to do the same, thought Blaney (*G.T.* 1903: 6).

If early Church of God writing endorsed giving, why did it oppose tithing? As E. E. Byrum put it, "Tithing was a doctrine and practise (*sic*) of the Old Testament, and is not of the New. Nowhere is it commanded or even recognized as a practice for New Testament saints" (*G.T.* 1904: 4). Of course, Byrum's radical interpretation of the New Testament led him to conclude that we must yield all that we have to God, not a mere tenth.

R. L. Berry, later a managing editor at the *Gospel Trumpet*, echoed Byrum's sentiments a dozen years later. The New Testament, he said, rested on a basis altogether different than the Old; love, not law, governed the giving of New Testament Christians. But Berry also encouraged giving to be regular, systematic, and as occasion required. Even so, Berry did not expect everybody to give. The "perfect equality" of the New Testament financial system saw to that: "If all were to give one tenth, it would be too hard on some and too easy on others. The New Testament system lays financial responsibility upon each according to his ability . . . The poor get all they need and the rich have nothing to waste" (*G.T.* 1915: 8).

Ten years later Berry had radically altered his stance. Tithing, he now said, rested on the principle that everything belonged to God and that the tithe was the portion set aside in recognition of God's sovereignty. As early as 1923 Berry had proposed a unified budget for the agencies. What accounted for Berry's change of mind? Two suggestions seem likely: (1) By 1925 the institutional ministry of the movement had enlarged considerably, five boards and agencies now needed regular giving on which to base their budgets; (2) as the unionization of American labor proceeded, the financial status of Church of God working people improved. Therefore, more money was available and, as a church, we were more capable of the kind of financial commitment required by the tithe system.

More research is needed on this period in our history. Why did we, a movement that once rejected tithing, come to accept the idea of the Associated Budgets and its successor, World Service? That and other such questions require answers. But in the meantime, it is enough for us to know of our forefathers' and foremothers' radical commitment to the principle of giving, and the identity of those to whom they gave.

Conflict and Camp Meeting

The words *camp meeting* call to mind annual meetings where powerful preaching, seasons of prayer and healing, and services of praise focus the hearts of those who attend. Overstating the importance of camp meetings in the life of the Church of God is almost impossible. From virtually the first of the great western camp meetings of the early 1800s, this institution of frontier Christianity became a fixture of popular piety. The camp meeting was so much a part of popular American Protestantism that early Church of God people naturally drew upon the camp meeting for inspiration and renewal. From that same source came much of their sense of the way to be the church.

As early as 1886 the camp meeting that convened nearest the Gospel Trumpet home was understood to be the movement's "general" camp meeting. In that year Bangor, Michigan, in Van Buren County and not too far from Grand Junction, was designated as the camp meeting for all the saints, everywhere. Announcing that meeting the *Trumpet* said, "It was a marvel of divine power and glory last year, and we expect the coming meeting to exceed in glory, all others, as the redeemed hosts have been much increased in numbers, and advanced in the power and fire of the Holy Spirit. Make your arrangements to come with a tent" (*G.T.* Apr. 15, 1886).

From towns and farms, cities and villages, the saints came to camp meeting. Along with their tents they carried other kinds of baggage—their fears and sicknesses, their joys and heartaches, their hopes and failures, their worries and their expectations. Perhaps we should not be surprised then, at the frequency and intensity of those occasions when camp meetings have become the arena of conflict.

In the spring of 1899 nobody in the movement fretted over the impending camp meeting more than E. E. Byrum. He had been editor of the *Gospel Trumpet* for four short years, having had no experience in publishing prior to that. In those days, the *Trumpet* and its editor held the movement together; great responsibility rested upon them to articulate the Spirit's leading.

The previous November, Byrum had dismissed from the Trumpet family some workers who had been teaching a heterodox form of the doctrine of sanctification. He had dubbed them "anti-cleansers" because their view implied that the believer's heart was not truly cleansed in the moment of entire sanctification. Many of the movement's preachers, some of them widely respected leaders such as W. A. Haynes, W. J. Henry and E. G. Masters, shared the viewpoint of the dismissed workers. As the 1899 camp meeting drew closer and closer, Byrum knew that conflict was likely. He took several steps to avoid an open dispute, but to no avail. The matter came to a head, and a sizable number of ministers left the movement.

To the Moundsville Camp Meeting of 1899 could be added several other camp meetings marked by conflicts large or small. After 1917 the General Assembly became the arena in which these typically have been expressed. From 1929 to 1934 the simmering conflict over Anderson College bubbled to the surface at Anderson

Camp Meeting more than once: F. G. Smith's defeated "Standard Literature" resolution, the assembly's rebuke of E. A. Reardon by voting him off the agency boards on which he sat, R. R. Byrum's heresy trial, Smith's failure at reelection by the Publication Board, and John Morrison's reratification by a margin of 13 votes.[4] One could add other periods and controversies to the list.

Why drag up all these incidents? Is there not something unseemly about conflict and controversy in the church? Is not this unseemliness even more inappropriate in a movement dedicated to a vision of the church as the seamless robe of Christ? Perhaps these questions can be at least partly answered in considering the church as an ongoing conversation about the meaning of the gospel for our lives. On this view, the church is a corporate, ongoing effort to answer the question, "What are the implications of the gospel for the living of our lives?" There is scarcely a more serious question for those whose great desire is to follow Jesus. As with most serious questions, this one is bound to call forth diverse answers. Such diversity, however, is not division and, moreover has the capacity to enrich the church's life. When diversity becomes division, we cross the line into schism. And schism sins against love—the love shed abroad in our hearts by the Spirit, the bond of perfectness.

Seeing Eye to Eye

In the fall of 1893 minor theological conflicts rippled through a portion of the Church of God ministry. D. S. Warner, editor of the *Gospel Trumpet* and the person at the heart of the movement, learned that some ministers were giving Matthew 19:23-26 a different reading than he. The text in question concerned Jesus' statement that a camel can sooner pass through the eye of a needle than the rich can enter the kingdom of heaven. Prior to joining the Church of God movement, some of our preachers had learned that one of the gates in Jerusalem's wall bore the name "Needle's Eye." From that bit of information they interpreted Jesus to mean that, although difficult, it was possible for the rich to be saved. Warner adhered to a literalist reading of the text. Jesus, said the editor, had said the eye of a needle and he meant the eye of a needle—not some gate in the city wall.

Another matter that caused concern at the Trumpet office involved reports that some of the saints were resorting to courts of law to solve problems with their neighbors. Others desired to use the courts but as yet had not. Both the desire and the actual use apparently contradicted the Apostle Paul's instruction. Rather than go to law, Warner said, we should (1) agree to settle with our adversaries, (2) be willing to suffer wrong, or (3) "take joyfully the spoiling of our goods." This was the plain teaching of Scripture.

Warner printed these conclusions in articles published in the *Gospel Trumpet* in December 1893 and January 1894. These articles carried similar titles, each of them insisting that the ministers of God must see "eye to eye." Warner's thoughts disclose more than his interpretations of biblical passages. They also illustrate his ideas about conflict in the church.

Apparently Warner more than merely disliked theological conflict within the ministry; he did not permit it. In his view, conflicts arose when ministers taught ideas that were sustained by the "traditions of sectism." "Only teach what you know by the sure Word and Spirit of God, and there will be harmony" (*G.T.* 1893: 4). Then, too, there was always the editor to ensure that ministers saw eye to eye, hence no conflict in the church. While conflict raged between the movement and those outside, inside harmony reigned.

As we know, even internal harmony did not endure. At least once in every generation since 1898 the movement has lived through deep conflicts and even schisms. What are we to make of these? What does their presence in our history say about us and our message of the unity of all Christians through the sanctifying Spirit? Should these episodes create a guilty conscience in the movement as a whole or in individual congregations whenever conflict emerges?

Warner eliminated conflict in two ways. First, he used the power of the editor's office to eliminate contrary opinion. The editor decided what material was printed in the *Trumpet*, and the power of such decisions prevented conflicting opinion from appearing in the paper. But what of personal conflict? Was Warner ever caught between a rock and a hard place? It seems not, and here we find the second means by which he eliminated conflict.

Warner's ministerial calling and his apprehension of what he called the Truth enabled him to transcend conflicting situations. His calling and the Truth served as criteria by which he judged these situations and disarmed problems. Indeed, when viewed from these criteria, conflict disappeared. This observation is borne out, sadly, in the second of Warner's three marriages, although neither of the first two could be called a success. Although he was concerned for his second wife Sarah's loneliness on the Nebraska prairie, Warner broke apart the conflicting pulls of marriage and ministry by answering his ministerial calling and always going out to preach. Their marriage suffered, Sarah's loneliness contributing to its deterioration. Warner ultimately sacrificed this marriage on the altar of the what he called the Truth. His wife could not abide his militant advocacy of the doctrine of the second blessing (or sanctification) and she left him. Conflict was resolved through a loyalty higher than marriage.

Following Warner's example, it may be that we can have a conflict-free movement or congregation. But such tranquility apparently will be purchased at a terribly high price. Is there no alternative road open to us? There may be, but we should not walk this road because we are unwilling to pay the heavy sacrifice required by Warner's way of transcending conflict. Rather we may recognize conflict to be a part of the historical life of people of God—Old Testament, New Testament, or 1893.

Quote from the Scripture that God blesses the righteous and punishes the wicked and then expect the psalmist to ask why it is that the wicked prosper. The point is not that such scriptural conflict makes both points of view untrue. Rather, the canon of Scripture makes impossible the human tendency to oversimplify it. We will not escape conflict by being "biblical people." Indeed, to be more biblical in our polity will likely increase our conflicts. For the people of God, conflict arises in living out the conviction that both are true. Thus those who struggle to live with conflicting truths also pay a price. But they do so in the communion of the saints and the presence of the Comforter.

So it may be the case that, concerning conflict in the church, we ought to have guilty consciences. But the guilt may be not in the fact that we have had conflict in the church, but in what we have done with it.

He Saw the Church

In the dark hours of April 24, 1947, a violent thunderstorm rumbled through Madison County, Indiana. At the south end of town nurses and nuns at St. John's-Hickey Memorial Hospital found the candles they knew they would need in the event of a power outage. One of those candles soon lit the room of F. G. Smith, who earlier had suffered a very serious heart attack. Only a year had passed since his return to Anderson with his wife, Birdie, to take up the demanding assignment of president of the Trumpet Company.

Agency president is a difficult assignment even during times of peace and tranquillity. But the 1940s were anything but peaceful in the Church of God. Two years before the Smiths moved to Anderson a bitter controversy had erupted in the movement. Agency leaders came under loud and sustained accusations for matters both real and imaginary: the movement was running down the road of "ecclesiasticism"; leading ministers were letting down the doctrinal standard by consulting physicians and attending movies; the agencies had become a power block that ran the movement without considering the grassroots church; too many of the same ministers sat on the boards of various agencies and these interlocking directorates concentrated power in the hands of a few. Whether or not these charges were true, simply that they existed illustrates the depths to which the level of trust had sunk by 1946.

Clearly, steps had to be taken to restore the movement's trust in its own ministerial leadership. Out of that concern F. G. Smith was asked to assume the presidency of the Gospel Trumpet Company and thereby help recreate a climate of trust and cooperation. Smith accepted the challenge and threw himself into the work. He crisscrossed the country, answering questions, allaying suspicions, dispelling rumors, listening to critics. But this grinding schedule proved too much for his heart. With Birdie, Dale and Polly Oldham, and Harold Phillips gathered about him in the candlelight, F. G. Smith passed away on that stormy April night.

"F. G.," as my students often refer to this man who died before most of them were born, had entered the ministry in 1898. That was the year Teddy Roosevelt and the Rough Riders charged up San Juan hill and the Anti-Cleansing heresy hit the Church of God.

Left to Right: F. G. Smith (1880-1947), E. E. Byrum (1861-1942), and Charles E. Brown (1883-1971). Each served as Editor in Chief of the Gospel Trumpet Company.

Smith served the work of the church in many capacities: personal secretary to E. E. Byrum, missionary, pastor, evangelist, and editor of the *Gospel Trumpet*. That last named position brought Smith great joy and bitter heartache. At an age when most men are in their prime, the editor was not reelected by the Publication Board.

One of the extraordinary characteristics of F. G. Smith—and there are many—is the attitude he took toward the loss of this position. Any of us can imagine a person, fallen from favor and no longer possessed of accustomed power, turning bitter, holding a grudge, and deciding to take his marbles and go home, but F. G. was not such a man.

Years after Smith left the editorial office and took a pastorate in Akron, Ohio, he and his editorial successor, C. E. Brown, found themselves together at a ministers' meeting in Springfield, Ohio. Everyone at that meeting knew that Smith and Brown differed in the way they saw the church, the former through the Book of Revelation and the latter through church history. Some young upstart decided to provoke an open fight between the two men and asked Brown whether he agreed with Smith. Every eye in the room fastened on the former editor as Brown answered.

"Freddie and I," said Brown, "are like two peddlers. He works his side of the street and I work mine." The audience broke out in laughter, the room's electric charge negated, and Smith did not challenge Brown's sage observation. In his editorial obituary of Smith, Brown lauded his predecessor's graciousness and his willingness to offer advice when it was solicited.

The authors of the important book, *Habits of the Heart*, say of American society, "For most of us, it is easier to think about how to get what we want than to know what exactly we should want" (Bellah 1985: 21). F. G. Smith mastered the difficult task of knowing what he should want. He set whatever personal setbacks he may have suffered against the larger backdrop of the movement and its common good. Smith knew that he should want that which served the common good of the church. We all can serve the common good whether at the head of the table or the foot. F. G. Smith understood that because he 'saw the church,' as we used to say, and gave himself to the realization of that vision.

Church of God Politics

Bill and Gloria Gaither have taught us all to sing about the church as the family of God. Like the families of which we have been a part, we often describe the church in the sentimental language of feelings. Both family and church engender deep emotions and attachments that should not be ignored or devalued. But these strong feelings tend to obscure the fact that family and church also are political groups.

Look through back issues of the *Gospel Trumpet*, particularly at volumes published around the year 1905, and you will find the following sentiments expressed in the "Letters" section of the paper:

"I am glad for the little Trumpet and read it with thanks and praise to God."

"I am happy every time I receive the paper and get to speak with the children of God with (*sic*) their letters."

"When the time nears for a new paper I long for it as for a dear friend."

"How blessed it is to hear those testimonies from east
to west."

In a very real sense, the *Gospel Trumpet/Vital Christianity* has
been the polity of the Church of God movement. Polity is simply
the term which means our "way of being together." Closely related
as it is to the word politics, defining polity as I have helps us
understand the futility of trying, as we often state, to "keep politics
out of the church." To do so is impossible, for if successful in that
goal we would eliminate our way of being together. Ironically,
when we attempt to keep politics out we consign ourselves to the
dirtiest forms of politics—those of secret telephone calls and back
room wheeling and dealing. What we want is not *no* politics but
good politics. As I say, the paper/magazine has served historically
as our way of being together.

The *Trumpet* served the movement as the means by which a geo-
graphically dispersed fellowship maintained contact with one
another. Readers found there information about the activities of
evangelists and the dates and locations of meetings. They read of
the joys and heartaches of the saints who testified through letters
published in the paper.

Similarly the *Trumpet* functioned to hold together little bands of
saints scattered all across the continent. So you might have read in
the *Trumpet* all sorts of information about the extended community.
Sometimes the news was mundane: folks in Belgrade, Minnesota,
reported trouble with the "itch." But other items reported much
more serious matters, as when editors warned readers that a member of the movement had fallen into heresy; the saints were forbidden any association or sympathy until the lapsed member's repentance and restoration.

The paper also counteracted the saints' social isolation. We often
forget some of the sadder consequences of "coming out" of sect
Babylon. For example, cases are reported of saints who were
refused the use of church buildings for funerals. These "come-outers" had forsaken the denominational congregation that owned the
building for a little band of Church of God people who often met in
someone's home. Such meeting places served well enough until
death visited the saints, some of whom naturally enough desired a

church building as the setting for a friend's or family member's funeral. But denominational congregations were understandably reluctant to share their buildings with those who labeled them as "Babel-confusion." In such instances of social deprivation the *Trumpet's* physical presence reminded readers that they, too, belonged to a people.

Still another dimension of the *Trumpet's* role in our polity is that the paper has served as the vehicle of our community. We have become accustomed to thinking of a community as a fellowship group, but more properly it is an extended conversation of a people about the implications of their traditions or narratives for their life together. The Church of God movement existed for more than 35 years before we had a general assembly to serve that function. Before—and since—1917 (the founding of the General Assembly), the *Trumpet* provided the means by which we conversed with one another. It was the place to publish one's convictions, try out new ideas, and re-affirm old ones.

The *Gospel Trumpet/Vital Christianity* has sustained the Church of God family because the movement possessed the virtues necessary to such a polity. Virtues like love, courage, and presence must exist among a people who want to be a movement rather than a denominational church. Only by displaying such virtues can it be a family that practices the good politics of the body of Christ. Because they are so important to our way of being together, the virtues of the people of God deserve our careful attention. Courage, love, and, especially, the virtue of presence turn out to be indispensable requirements for the polity of the church. Apart from their display the church is not the church at all, but something utterly alien to Paul's vision of the body of Christ.

The Glue That Holds Us Together

I have often observed and said that the Gospel Trumpet Company, publishing house of the Church of God movement, has provided its way of being together, its polity, for much of the movement's history. Furthermore, I have stated that certain virtues are necessary for a church that has such a polity.

If I might slightly alter my metaphors here, the publications of the Gospel Trumpet Company/Warner Press have been the pot that contains the glue that has held together the rich and diverse fellowship called the Church of God movement. That glue is composed of several elements, but three in particular are the moral virtues of love, courage, and presence.

In the church we have talked a great deal of love, and I'm not about to repeat those well-known observations here. Love is the "bond of perfectness" after all, which "unites us all in Jesus." Love is not the warm fuzzy of good fellowship, but the power of God that keeps you in the church—even with people you do not necessarily like. One of our very best songs, D. S. Warner's "Bond of Perfectness," amply illustrates the central importance of love in the glue that holds us together. But the Beatles were wrong; love is not all you need.

Courage is another indispensable ingredient in the glue that holds us together. A community is an extended conversation about the implications of the narratives of God, Jesus, Israel, and the church. For the community called the church this is no idle conversation, but our determined effort to discern the kind of people God is calling us to be. Since that is the case, we must have leadership possessed of the courage to tell us what it really thinks. Moreover, this leadership must be courageous enough to listen to the tiniest voice among us who also has the courage to speak. We must have courage to change and courage to recognize the good idea put forth by someone else.

While much could be said of the virtues of love and courage, I want to focus my attention on the virtue of "presence." The arrival of the *Trumpet* reminded the saints of their community's presence. This is crucial, for without the touch of another, without someone's presence, our souls begin to dry. So it is that, at our moment in the movement's history, the virtue of presence may be even more important than either love or courage (if they are separable), because to the degree that we fail to be present in each other's lives the glue that holds us together begins to dry and crack.

The polity of the Church of God has been an extremely fragile process. It is highly relational in character and, therefore, dependent upon the presence of one another to each other. Our polity requires the mutual experiencing of one another. We trust our experience of you, as it were, and once we have experienced you we'll let you do and say some rather astounding things. Why?—because you have been present; you have allowed your soul to be touched, and you have touched our souls.

For the first thirty-seven years of its existence, the Gospel Trumpet Company ate and lived in one another's presence. The legacy of the practice of that virtue partially sustained the company through years of economic depression and wartime shortages. The same legacy sustained young agencies and their leaders, who also practiced the virtue of presence in the church—eating in one another's kitchens, sleeping in one another's homes, and staying for the whole meeting even when they were not on the program.

If the glue that holds us together has begun to dry and crack, then it only stands to reason that a renewal of the virtues of love, courage, and presence may warm that glue and restore its bonding power. But especially we need presence—the presence that cuts across administrative flow charts; a presence that flows through and across the church; a presence to one another inside the agencies and congregations in which we worship and work. A renewal of the virtue of presence will mean more "management by walking around," not because it is a technique recommended by the latest management study but because our souls are nourished through their presence to one another in the midst of the Spirit.

Among the human soul's unique properties is its sensitivity to the presence of another, especially through its capacity to be touched. The soul learns two reactions—the cold fear of recoil from the hostile touch and the warm extension of the soul to the one who reaches out in kinship. If we can recapture the virtue of presence, if it can permeate our work in the church, then perhaps the warmth of another's presence will warm the glue that holds us together. Inestimably, that glue is warmed by the fire of the Presence in whom our souls take delight.

A New Social Imagination

During the life of any enduring religious movement events of an unusual significance occur. Such moments capture the essence of an individual's or group's commitments in a way which fundamen-

93

tally defines that group's ordering of reality. The events create a paradigm, a way of organizing and interpreting our experience.

Moments of such significance that they shape our way of construing the world may properly be called "paradigmatic events." The first of two paradigmatic events in the life of the Church of God movement occurred in the spring of 1881. Actually, this event took place before the movement had even begun. Nevertheless, D. S. Warner's experiences during that spring profoundly shaped his vision of the church. His views shaped the movement's conceptions. Thus the events of that spring gave him and the movement a paradigm through which they—and we—have "seen the church."

Late in April, 1881, Warner held a revival meeting at Hardinsburg, Indiana. While there he spent an entire day praying about a matter which had been troubling his spirit for some time. As Warner later reported in the Gospel Trumpet, "The Spirit of the Lord showed me the inconsistency of repudiating sects and yet belonging to an association that is based on sect recognition" (G.T. 1881:2). The inconsistency to which Warner referred was his own. For some time he had preached against the division of the church into a collection of competing denominations, which he called the "sect-system." But Warner also belonged to the Indiana State Holiness Association, a loose association of holiness evangelists that insisted that its members belong to some denomination. Warner could no longer resolve the contradiction in which he lived. No longer could he participate in an association which implicitly endorsed the denominational separation of Christians he was otherwise attacking. Warner refused to abide any longer the self-contradiction whereby he preached against rules for membership in the church while belonging to an organization that m,ade such rules.

On May 20-21, 1881 Warner attended the Holiness Association's meeting in Terre Haute, Indiana. He took with him a proposal to amend the association's bylaws. If amended, they would no longer require denominational membership as a necessary prerequisite of association membership. If the association were to accept Warner's amendment, its membership would be opened "to all true Christians everywhere" (June 1, 2). The association defeated Warner's proposal, however. Within a very short time he withdrew from its fellowship.

This is a paradigmatic event, alongside a similar withdrawal at Beaver Dam only a few months later, because it so profoundly shaped Warner and the movement's conception of the church and its membership. He had been preaching and writing ideas about the church. As a consequence of his rejection at Terre Haute, Warner now had to live out those ideas in a new way. The early leaders' ideas about the church had to be incarnated in a new way of being the church. The Terre Haute events helped them arrive at a new paradigm of the church.

Sometimes Church of God people erroneously conclude that this paradigm means that we oppose church membership. That is not quite correct; we oppose all *human* requirements for membership in the church. But God requires all members of the church to be born again. Those who follow Jesus as Lord and Master are members of the church and may refer to themselves as "members." This way of construing the reality of our experience in Christ has provided the Church of God movement with its way of being the church. Warner would not abide any human conditions as a litmus test of his membership in the holiness association. Such membership ought to be predicated, in his view, on the grounds that one was a true Christian and on those grounds alone.

This paradigmatic event led Warner to exercise what Old Testament scholar Walter Brueggemann calls a "social imagination." Writing about the Israelites of Exodus and the Babylonian exile, Brueggemann describes their social imagination as "a poetic, imaginative proposal for a community of the marginal who are able to envision a different shape for life" (1987:43). This imagination is a "new ability, courage, and will to hope, imagine, design, and implement alternative scenarios of how it could be" (20). Israel looked for the new thing that Yahweh would do in its midst. Out of this new thing in Israel a new community unlike anything in Israel's past waited to be born. To discern its shape required an exercise in imagination, and a new paradigm.

D. S. Warner's experience was roughly akin to Israel's. Like Israel, he found himself on the margins of his society; he knew little of wealth, power, and influence. He also suffered the pain that comes in the discovery that one is an outcast. But through the mysterious workings of God, his marginalized position and his pain combined to cause him to reject the American religious *status quo*, the business-as-usual way of denominational religion. Warner's social imagination worked in him the vision of a "church beyond division," as C. E. Brown later named it. In such a church Christians would live free of all humanly contrived rules and regulations about who may or may not be a member. It was a daring vision in 1881, and not very many people shared it, but those who did claimed that they had "seen the church."

The vision of the early leaders of the Church of God movement remains a challenge for us. This vision dares us to stand against the constant temptation to define by our own standards who may and who may not be a member of the church. To yield to that temptation is to look for a new paradigm, and consequently no longer see the church as we once did.

The Inspired Community

Early in 1886, the congregation meeting at Prospect Chapel in Jay County, Indiana, closed out a revival meeting. According to C. E. Brown these earnest persons still sought "more light" (1951: 123). Shortly afterward, D. S. Warner and his evangelistic company rode into town. They started another meeting, and among those who came out of denominational Christianity was Henry C. Wickersham.

Henry Wickersham was born May 19, 1850 in Randolph County, Indiana. At the age of sixteen he experienced conversion and joined the United Brethren Church. In 1872 he married Clara Walters, and their union produced eight children. Their daughter Della married A. L. Byers, the biographer of D. S. Warner. After Wickersham entered the fellowship of the Church of God, he offered the movement his considerable skills as a speaker and writer. He pastored the congregation at Praise Chapel, where many of his relatives in the Byrum family worshiped. In fact, it was Henry Wickersham who mentioned his nephew, E. E. Byrum, to Warner as a potential purchaser of a half-interest in the *Gospel Trumpet* in 1887. Later Wickersham entered evangelistic work and was instrumental in the early ministerial training of C. E. Orr and C. W. Naylor. In 1916 Wickersham died as the result of a sudden illness. J. T. Wilson traveled over from Anderson to Praise Chapel to conduct Wickersham's funeral. Wickersham was buried in the adjoining cemetery.

Wickersham was at the center of the movement's life and thought. He wrote two books during his ministry, *Holiness Bible Subjects* and *History of the Church*. The second of these is a useful source of information about the movement's earliest days, written by a man who was both an eyewitness to and a participant in many of those events. Wickersham's position at the center of the movement lends credibility to his ideas.

In *Holiness Bible Subjects*, Wickersham had this to say about the Bible: "It is the men who wrote the Bible that were inspired. Inspiration acts not on the man's words, not on the man's thought, but on the man himself" (1894:18-19). Wickersham thought that the Holy Spirit inspired *people*, not words. In fact, he expressly stated that inspiration is not of words or even thoughts—but people. Since Wickersham focused his attention on inspired people, it is fair to interpret the subject of his statement to be the church as much as it is the Bible.

I mention Wickersham's ideas because of their interesting and useful perspective on the church. We may infer from Wickersham's statement that he thought that the church was an inspired community. That is to say, inspiration is a matter, first and foremost, of the Spirit's presence as the illuminating, animating, guiding presence in the church. If we agree with Paul that the church is the body of Christ, then it would only make sense to think of the Holy Spirit as the soul of that body. This is but another way of saying "inspiration."

Open the pages of many an early Gospel Trumpet Company publication and you will find in the preface a sentence that testifies that the Holy Spirit led the writer to set down the contents of the book. Early Church of God writers could say this because they believed, with Wickersham, that "inspiration acts on the man himself." This belief should not be interpreted to mean that they did not think Scripture was unique; they clearly did. But they did not ground their understanding of that uniqueness in a doctrine of inspired words. Inspiration acts "on the man himself." In this sense, that early Church of God people thought the church was inspired, a people animated by the breath of the Spirit, seems quite clear.

Henry (1850-1916) and Clara Wickersham and their family. An uncle of Gospel Trumpet editor E. E. Byrum, Henry Wickersham was among the first converts to the Church of God movement in east central Indiana and pastor of the congregation at Praise Chapel.

The idea of the church as an inspired community holds promise for our life and thought as the people of God today. When the church gathers for worship, God is not over against us, an external object out there to be praised. Rather, the Spirit inspires the worshiping community as the very source of its life and unity. As they join in this act of God-inspired praise, the people of God engage in a world-making enterprise.

In reference to Israel's book of praise, the Psalms, Walter Brueggemann says, "In public worship Israel is engaged in constructing a world in which Israel can viably, joyously, and obediently live" (1988:6). As the people of God praise God, they go about the all-important work of putting together a world of relationships to God, the creation (including people), and the larger society that form the very fabric that clothes their lives.

When H. C. Wickersham set down his idea of inspiration, he set before us a notion of an inspired community quite in keeping with Brueggemann's description of Israel. The two visions share an appreciation of the role of the corporate life of the people of God. We do not have either the right or the privilege of enforcing our private opinion as the will of the whole. The Spirit is not the private property of a man or a woman. The Spirit breathes through the whole people of God. But this will be seen as clearly necessary when we consider the enormous scope of the world-constructing task toward which the Spirit drives us. It is a world of relationships the likes of which this old world has never seen and can barely fathom. It is a world where justice gushes and the flash-flood of righteousness bathes every one of us, and none will be denied.

Early Church of God writers may not have used such language, but their testimony to the illuminating presence of the Spirit says that they thought of the church as an inspired community. It is now our turn to hold this jewel to the light, turning it to expose new facets which will guide us. It is not for us to parrot the sayings of our forefathers and foremothers. We are to be an inspired community, a congregation that praises God. This praise is both the end and the beginning. It is the end because its aim is God. It is the beginning because praise engages us in the task of constructing a world that witnesses to the justice, righteousness, and goodness of God.

The Restoration of Babel

Those who read only superficially the early literature of the Church of God movement nevertheless will likely encounter the word, *Babel*. It refers, of course, to the famous story recorded in Genesis 11. When the earth's inhabitants spoke but one language, the men who lived in the plain of Shinar set themselves to building a tower that would touch heaven itself. But human arrogance and the prospect of even greater and mightier deeds at their hands displeased the Lord. So he multiplied their languages, thereby scattering them over the face of the earth, and their tower-building came to an end. This forlorn city and its tower were given the name Babel, "because there the Lord confused the language of all the earth" (Gen. 11:9, RSV).

Babel means confusion, and from that definition early Church of God preachers and writers launched sharp, polemical darts at the confused state of denominational Christianity which they termed the "sect system." Thus D. S. Warner termed denominations the "dark picture of present-day sect confusion," and drew a clear analogy between the dwellers of Shinar and the people of Warner's own time whom the Lord had similarly confounded and divided from one another (*The Church of God*, n.d.: 14). Furthermore, in that same tract Warner rhetorically asked whether "the members of the sects have the same care for one another" (14). This question implies that Warner believed that "Babel confusion" pre-empted the possibility of such care. Just as denominational Christianity's confusion created a multiplicity of fellowships and doctrinal voices, so this confusion also forestalled the possibility of genuine, mutually intelligible caring among people. Only in the true church, Warner seems to have thought, would Christians find the care that originates in brotherly and sisterly love.

In the century and more since Warner suggested that genuine care can be found among those who faithfully follow their Lord, dozens of institutions of caring have been founded by men and women of the Church of God movement. People of the Church of God have founded schools, hospitals and medical missions from Kenya to Brazil to Japan. One thinks of homes for the aged or those who otherwise are unable to live alone, and homes come to mind in places like South Haven, Michigan; St. Paul Park, Minnesota; Anderson, Indiana; and Roanoke, Virginia. To mention homes for children and youth conjures up recollections of such institutions in such widespread locales as Grand Junction, Michigan, and Cuttack, India; one also thinks of youth ranches and farms in Washington, Colorado, and Kentucky. In the years immediately following World War II the Church of God movement also sponsored the re-settlement in the United States and Canada of hundreds of "displaced persons" who were uprooted during the war years.

The mention of such institutions and acts, and many others could also be cited, does not yet even begin to touch the depths of hospitality poured out to fellow believers in missionary homes or parsonages. Nor can we begin to estimate the number of homes opened by lay people to traveling evangelists, college quartets and trios, and countless others. Each of these expresses some act of

Christian caring for another, but my attention is drawn particularly to those institutions which have focused their attention and care on those who were, or are, without a home—the orphanages and shelters, the youth ranches, and the homes for the elderly.

Warner thought that "Babel confusion" forestalled the possibility of genuine caring in the church. He may have taken an excessively dim view of denominational Christianity, but the principle he detected remains worth noting. Babel means confusion. Think of the panic that raced through Babel's streets when unknown and unrecognizable utterances began falling on the resident's ears. Imagine the confused din of panic swelled by shouting people straining to communicate with others who might as well have been deaf. In such fear, people are overwhelmed by the need to make themselves understood; what assumes paramount importance is *to make somebody understand me.* Warner believed the world of denominational Christianity to be crippled by the same preoccupation; everybody straining to speak the loudest, few if any silent listeners attentive to the voice of another. In the noise of Babel the voice surest to be lost, so Warner seems to have thought, is the weakest, the one most likely to be overlooked even in the best circumstance, the voice that belongs to those Jesus called "the least of these." The ruckus kicked up by Babel confusion drowned out the cry of the needy.

The good news, of course, which Warner and the early Church of God movement announced is that "from the yokes of Babel's lords from henceforth we are free." The church is the sign and tangible expression of God's undoing of the confusion of Babel. In the words of theologian Stanley Hauerwas, the church is the "people of God's time, and we rejoice in the knowledge that we are not condemned to repeat the past. That means that we really do have an alternative to Babel, to fear of one another, and finally then to war. Even more happily it means that insofar as we are the church, we do not just have an alternative, we are the alternative. We do not have a story to tell but in the telling we *are* the story being told" (1988: 54).

The church, then, is God's new language. People need not live in the confused, self-preoccupied din of Babel. As seen by D. S. Warner and countless other men and women of the Church of God movement, the church speaks God's new language as it performs the scriptures. Therefore, who we are, and the actions that proceed from that character, may finally be of much greater importance that what we say. Warner seems to have been convinced that acts of Christian charity illustrate—no, they are tangible expressions of the church, the alternative to Babel confusion.

Chapter Three Notes

1. Barry Callen has compiled several sources of information about the origin and historic actions of the General Assembly. These can be found in *The Assembly Speaks*, 1985.

2. Additional information about the National Association of the Church of God can be found in *The National Association of the Church of God Historical Report, 1917-1974*, n.d.; and Wilfred Jordan & Richard Willowby, Eds., *The National Association of the Church of God: Diamond Jubilee*, 1991.

3. The two most extended treatments of this episode can be found in John A. Morrison's autobiography, *As the River Flows*, 1962, and Robert H. Reardon, *The Early Morning Light*, 1979.

4. These events are woven together by Robert Reardon in *The Early Morning Light*, (Anderson: Warner Press, 1979).

Families (4)

Marriage for Good Reasons

One of the first members of the Church of God in Muskogee, Oklahoma was a German-American nursery-man by the name of Joe Kreiner. Until middle age Joe lived the life of a bachelor. But about that time his attitude toward marriage changed. Evidently the Muskogee Church did not have many women who met the qualifications Joe had for his as yet unknown bride-to-be. For he found it necessary to advertise for a German-speaking Christian lady through the *Gospel Trumpet*. A women from Texas answered the ad. She and Joe were married and they actively participated in the life of the church in Muskogee for many years.

Somehow this charming little story does not fit the notions of love and marriage that circulate, particularly at St. Valentine's day. How did our forefathers and mothers think about marriage anyway?

J. Grant Anderson (1873-1927) took up questions of home and domestic life in his 1921 book, *Sex Life and Home Problems*. Anderson grew up near Union City, Pennsylvania, and came into the Church of God movement through the ministry of H. M. Riggle. In 1903, Anderson was ordained, and he subsequently pastored congregations in Philadelphia and Franklin, Pennsylvania.

Several preachers and writers in the Church of God movement believed that their ministries extended to publishing their reflections and insights on domestic and family relationships. Among the early contributors to this literature was J. Grant Anderson (1873-1927), a popular preacher who served congregations in Philadelphia and Franklin, Pennsylvania.

Anderson devoted a considerable block of his time to evangelistic work. His book of domestic advice remained in print and sold particularly well in the 1930s.

Anderson said some interesting things about "who may safely marry." Neither parental dictates nor statutes, not even love provided safe criteria. Physiology, in which Anderson had a considerable interest, suggested that the age of marriage might coincide with the beginning of the ability to conceive and bear children. But he modified physiological criteria with the requirement of maturity. Young people, said Anderson, were better off to wait until age 20 or 21 before marrying (1921: 64).

Anderson wanted people to marry "safely." What did he mean by a safe marriage? It turns out that he was thinking primarily of the kind of children the proposed marriage would produce. Marriages between the immature, persons suffering from "hereditary diseases," or those past their reproductive prime tended to produce weak or abnormal children, according to Anderson's book.

Admittedly, Anderson's understanding of physiology was mistaken in some points. Physical condition, more than age, affects pregnancy and fetal development. But beyond his dated ideas about that, Anderson articulated an idea of marriage quite different from the standard fare of today. Marriage, thought Anderson, enabled the development of the individual, promoted the welfare of society and perpetuated the species. None of that sounds very romantic. But then Anderson understood marriage more as a social-economic-political institution of much more weight than mere romance. Certainly he thought more of marriage than the modern day notion that it is a mutual agreement for self-fulfillment and "happiness."

Today people, especially the young but not only them, marry for love, because it seems like the right thing to do at the time. They look to their partner for their own fulfillment. J. Grant Anderson did not understand marriage that way at all. Thus he could offer reasons why people should or should not marry. Most of us would be hard-pressed to come up with any justification beyond "love," and rather vaguely stated notions of that.

Please do not misunderstand me. Love surely is important, indeed crucial, to marriage. But Anderson's view of marriage may have something very important to contribute to ours. This may be particularly true of his assumption that one of the reasons for marriage is having children. Then there also is Anderson's understanding of the economic and political dimensions of marriage. That, too, may instruct us.

Marriage, it turns out is more than an act of love and passion, more than a mutual contract to provide another's happiness. Men and women should enter into this institution for good reasons and out of sober judgment. Maybe that's why Joe Kreiner could do such an unromantic thing as advertise for a wife. Seems odd to us. But then, that marriage endured.

"Home, Health, and Success"

People looking for early Church of God movement attitudes toward matters like abortion need look no further than Thomas Nelson's *Home, Health, and Success.* This collection of advice about matters domestic and economic had been translated from the Dano-Norwegian original, *Hjem, Helbred, og Lykke,* in 1907. Readers could find in its pages recommendations for proper marriage companions, child-rearing, "how and when to eat and drink", and the like. Nelson also discussed such confidential matters as birth control, conception, and pregnancy. In this connection he offered his judgment on abortion.

Thomas Nelson (1872-1946) was born on the island of Mors, Denmark and sailed to the United States sometime between the ages of fourteen and nineteen. We know very little of his boyhood. In the summer of 1893, Nelson experienced conversion, and within two more years he claimed entire sanctification. By some as yet unknown route, Nelson's religious pilgrimage carried him into the Church of God movement. Together with another gospel worker named Charlie Akers, Nelson conducted evangelistic meetings in association with the Church of God January 13-22, 1895, at Fairport, Iowa. The men described themselves as "both young and new in the work (*G.T.* 1895: n.p.).

Nelson's name appeared in the *Trumpet* field reports increasingly after 1900. By then he had co-edited a collection of hymns and gospel songs published in Dano-Norwegian. He reported evangelistic tours among the Scandinavian immigrants who had settled in the areas surrounding Hutchinson, Norway Lake, and Irving, Minnesota. These activities demonstrate Nelson's growing sense that God was calling him to ministry among the tens of thousands of Scandinavian immigrants of the upper Midwest. In time, Nelson became the editor of a Scandinavian language publishing house and the guiding spirit among several like-minded Scandinavian-Americans. During the first quarter of the twentieth century and on the slenderest of resources, this small group founded and operated the publishing house, a missionary home, and the first incorporated Old People's Home in the Church of God. They were truly a remarkable group of people, and Thomas Nelson's deep dedication to their work gave them a strong leader.

In *Home, Health, and Success* Nelson offered his opinion about abortion. He called it "the most cruel and low-down practise (*sic*) and the most beastly crime that the world has ever known" (1907: 105). Nelson opposed abortion, not on the grounds that unborn children are "persons" or because they possessed some right, but because "God . . . counts . . . the unborn from the moment they are begotten, or from the moment conception takes place" (107). Of course, in 1907 abortion was also illegal, meaning that the woman who sought to end a pregnancy likely placed her own life in the hands of an unlicensed and dangerous practitioner. Nelson also feared for the health and safety of women driven to such desperation.

Nelson's theology of marriage left no place for abortion and precious little room for birth control. He approached the matter of contraception from a moral point of view that I would describe as falling loosely within natural law ethics. According to this ethical position a close parallel exists between divine law and the natural order. Actions contrary to nature are therefore also judged to violate God's intentions. Thus Nelson wrote, "We need hardly ask whether such [contraception] is right or wrong; for it stands to reason that it is always wrong to break the laws of God (104). Nelson hastened to add that he did not think that women should be forced to bear children every other year of their marriages, but he did think that additional children in a marriage already possessed of them were desirable. I find it very interesting, in this connection, that Nelson associated contraception with "high society," in effect applying a rough socio-economic twist to his argument. The wealthy and morally suspect upper-class practiced contraception, whereas a more virtuous yeoman and small-town class did not think themselves above God's natural law; the larger families of rural America thus were, in Nelson's eyes, the divinely appointed norm.

Like the Roman Catholic moral theological tradition, Nelson believed that procreation was one of the central purposes of marriage. More than simply desirable, the production and proper rearing of children "is the first and primary duty or work of every married man or woman" (109). Such a conservative view of marriage clearly departs from modern notions. This view also challenges some of the assumptions of those notions. The modern idea of marriage assumes, for example, that two people are free to choose the kind of marriage they desire. By insisting that procreation is a necessary part of marriage, Nelson asserted that marriage comes with certain expectations, that those who marry are not free to use this institution to satisfy their own predetermined list of desires.

Nelson's views also raise very serious questions about marriage and the reasons Christians marry and have children. It seems to me that such reasons, if they can be established, might have something to say about Christians' attitudes toward abortion. For example, do Christians think differently about marriage and procreation than those who are not followers of Jesus? Does our discipleship make any difference in our decisions to marry and have children? If such differences do exist, what are they? What are the consequences of those differences for the way Christians think about abortion?

We need not agree with Thomas Nelson's conclusions about abortion in order to appreciate the fact that his Christian discipleship clearly influenced his thought. In fact, I find this connection between discipleship and social policy rather refreshing. I seem to hear in this connection the breeze of the Spirit who desires that all of us will live within God's shalom, that comprehensive peace that passes all understanding.

Church and Family

The early Church of God movement rather easily interchanged ideas of family and church. Sometimes families acted like the church; at other times the church acted like a family. That observation begs to be enlarged with a discussion of examples of early Church of God attitudes toward families.

Before the turn of the century, in the days of the flying messengers, Sebastian and Chloe Michels founded a children's home at Grand Junction, Michigan. He did not originally intend this home to be an orphanage, and in its first years of operation it was not. The Michels' chief concern was for the care and well-being of children of the flying messengers. Should children be expected to share the rigors and, sometimes, the dangers of travel? On the other hand, should the movement get into the business of building chil-

The children's home at Grand Junction, Michigan, founded by Sebastian and Chloe Michels.

dren's homes for gospel workers? After all, a home for children would require, sooner or later, means for their schooling.

The Michels' answered such questions by starting a children's home in 1893. The concern for schooling had been answered a year earlier; later a building was put up for that purpose and still remains on the Grand Junction camp grounds. Sebastian and Chloe became the managers of the home, which received the voluntary services of others such as C. E. Orr and Nora Siens (later, Hunter). Within a few years the home was enlarged to include the charitable care of orphaned children.

The Michels' concern for children is gratifying, but not particularly noteworthy. After all, we expect Christians to be aware of and speak to the needs of others, especially children. What I find interesting in this little episode is the attitude of the flying messengers toward their own children. They must have been willing to leave their children in the care of others, sometimes for rather lengthy periods of time. Why would they do such a thing? How could they?

I think it is too easy to say that the flying messengers were extraordinarily committed to the truths of the reformation. That is undoubtedly true, but I do not believe they therefore were willing to sacrifice their children to the movement. The flying messengers who left their children at the Grand Junction home trusted their children into Sebastian and Chloe Michels' care. That is worth remembering; some members of the church possessed such depths of trust that it enabled them to place their children in the care of other members of the church. But people do not trust blindly concerning the welfare of their children. The flying messengers did not simply believe that their children would be all right. No, they trusted Sebastian and Chloe, Charles and Nora, and all the others who cared for their children. The messengers had confidence in the character of the people in whom the care of their children had been entrusted.

Could it also be possible that the messengers did not think of their children as their possessions? Perhaps they thought of children as God's gift to the whole church, a promise of the future. If children are such a gift, then everyone in the church at one time or another may find himself or herself caring for these gifts. And if children are God's gift (as we often piously repeat at their births and dedications), may we ever think of them as possessions? If we thought of children as God's gift to the church, signs of hope, then perhaps we would find it more difficult to take from some children and give to others simply because some are *ours* and others are *theirs*. If it became more difficult for us to justify such actions would that not be good for all of us?

Families and the Church

The photograph collection in the Archives of the Church of God contains an interesting portrait of a woman named, simply, "Mother" O'Brien. She was the laundress for the Gospel Trumpet Company at Moundsville. "Brother" and "Sister" of course are familiar titles to many in the movement, and "Mother" was a title that had been given to Sarah Smith. That the term also applied to Mother O`Brien makes me wonder how widespread was the early Church of God practice of honoring women by referring to them as "Mother." Additionally, were any men honored by the title "Father" as in the sense of "Father Abraham?"

Those last two questions aside, the use of such titles points to

"Mother" O'Brien, laundress for the Gospel Trumpet Company during its years in Moundsville, West Virginia (1898-1907).

the importance of the family as a model for early Church of God social life. The Gospel Trumpet Company's early communalism illustrates the point. Workers earned no salaries, whether linotype operators or company officers. All lived in the same quarters, the Trumpet home. Female workers in need of new clothing made a request of the home matron, who authorized a clothing draw from common stores; male workers went through the home manager. Cash for emergencies could be requested through the same channels. "Trumpet family" meals were eaten, appropriately, family style. Given the context, one certainly can understand the use of titles like mother, brother, and sister. The communal and multigenerational Gospel Trumpet Company functioned something like an extended family. At least in Grand Junction, Moundsville, and for the first few years in Anderson, the Trumpet home and the missionary homes functioned like families. We could say that in such instances family served as an important model for church.

Families also acted like churches. Early Church of God families were encouraged to worship together. The Gospel Trumpet Company sold plaques and wall mottoes with which people could decorate their homes. Christian decor replaced worldly. A good deal of printed opinion also encouraged house worship. But worship in the home comprised more than a story from *Egermeier's* with a short prayer afterward. There was *singing* and reading of the Scripture itself followed by *exposition* of the text by a parent. At least, that was the recommended practice.

All of this suggests that "family" and "church" were ideas that cross-fertilized each other in the early decades of the Church of God movement. Family relationships served as models of the ideal relationship between Christians. *Family* practices were institutionalized at the Trumpet home. *Church* practices of prayer, preaching, and worship were encouraged in the family setting. Family settings were seen as appropriate for church functions. In other words, the line separating family and church activities was not at all clear in the early days of the Church of God movement.

Today we place much higher expectations on the family and church. One of the things we expect our churches to do, for example, is "save the family." It may be unfair to expect so much of the church. For one thing, the family of the 1990s is not the family of 1905. It is unrealistic to think that the nuclear families of contemporary North America can perform all the functions of extended families of a by-gone era. Yet we put great pressure on our nuclear families to do precisely that—and more.

One wonders how the blurred line between family and church in our history might speak to their interrelationship in our own time.

Families and More

In November of 1907, not far from St. James, Missouri, Tom Morrison and Amanda Martin were married. Both of them were widowed, which in this case meant that Tom brought seven children into this union and Amanda, three. To this brood of ten, Tom and Amanda added three more girls. In today's terminology they would be called a "blended" family.

One of Tom's seven children was a fourteen-year-old boy named John, as in John A. Morrison, future president of Anderson College. One of Amanda's three was also a fourteen-year-old, Earl, as in Earl L. Martin, future dean of the School of Theology at Anderson College. Earl and John finished their adolescent years as step-brothers. Although not related by blood, they were indeed brothers, and close.

A large family living in cramped quarters on a horse trader's income was bound to strain the bonds of love and forgiveness. The day came when Earl had taken all he could. So he saddled up a horse and rode down the hollow, away from home, straight to Billy Beezley's farm. Billy and John were related on his late mother's side of the family; Billy and Earl were not related at all. But that did not prevent Billy from opening his home. Maybe the boy's hot meals there were seasoned with some sage advice. Two days later, Earl rode home.

A few years later Earl and John managed to fall in love simultaneously. They would have had a double wedding except that Earl got sick. John and Eunice Drenner, like Earl, were teachers and the leaves of absence they had taken were about to expire, so they proceeded with their plans. Five days later Earl and Blanch Williams followed the Morrisons into matrimony. All four of them made a home together. Blanch kept the house and cooked while the other three taught school. That was September 1912.

From a much later perspective, these stories seem quaint and a bit foreign. Few newlyweds would even pause to consider such living arrangements. Surely the Morrisons' and Martins' poor financial circumstances forced them into this abnormal domestic economy. The lack of money may have figured in their decision. But, then, today's nuclear family was not the norm in 1912. Certainly it was not the norm in the Morrison-Martin tribe. Their living arrangement likely did not strike them as oddly as it does us.

Nuclear families are really a modern invention and tied rather closely to an industrial or increasingly post-industrial economy. This kind of family is now expected to carry burdens formerly shared by extended families. But the nuclear family is incapable of carrying such a load. Fewer and fewer Uncle Billys are down the road, with a light on for the runaways of our time.

Some of this we have brought on ourselves, with our incessant mobility and dedication to careers. This makes us ready to make "career moves" and tear the web of relationships that are woven among extended families and neighbors that occupy the same general space called home. This dislocation is good neither for neighborhoods nor children who are thereby forced to grow up far away from grandparents.

Parents' Duties to Their Children

When Christians think of children in the context of the church, sooner or later the subject will likely turn to Sunday schools. It is of course the case that Sunday schools are intended as much for adults as for children, but we nevertheless tend to connect them primarily with youngsters. Very early in the life of the Church of God movement we opposed "Sabbath schools," as they were then often called. The care of children was not the issue. Rather, early Church of God people did not trust the Sunday school system structured by denominational churchgoers. No scriptural warrant could be found to support the idea of Sunday schools (always a powerful argument among Church of God people), and they were also regarded as "hotbeds of pride and false religion" (*G.T.* 1 Dec. 1885: 1).

The religious training of the young mattered very much to our forefathers and foremothers. They just happened to think that the home provided the best setting for this instruction. The family constituted a miniature congregation, presided over by the parents. Houses substituted for church buildings. Instead of expensive paintings and other extravagant adornment, homes were recommended to be furnished with religious mottoes and "good religious books." The Gospel Trumpet Company offered an ample supply of both.

Poets and musicians wrote songs especially for house worship, which was encouraged as a daily practice. No ritual was prescribed, but the elements of prayer, Bible reading, and singing occurred "as the Spirit led." Children as young as three were believed to be mature enough to listen to the reading and explanation of small sections of Scripture. Little ones could receive "divine impressions" at a surprisingly early age; parents therefore were to begin the religious training of their children while they were yet infants. As the saying goes, as the twig is bent, so grows the tree.

The early Church of God movement's thought concerning children in families ranged far beyond the matters of religious instruction. The movement's writers ventured opinions on a wide variety of topics. Marriages, for example, that lacked the intention to produce children were considered "carnal" and unfit homes for any children that such unions might accidentally produce. Family planning, however, did receive the early movement's blessing, and writers sometimes even explained methods of birth control for their adult readers. Nevertheless, men and women of the Church of God movement expected that, sooner or later, children would be born into families that were not prevented from childbearing by some medical condition.

Once born, children were completely at the disposal of their parents. After all, they bore the responsibility for whoever emerged on the other side of childhood and adolescence. That belief meant that the best interests of the child required him or her (in those days children often were called "it") to be governed rather than govern: "Parents are not to be in subjection to the children, but the children are to be subject to the parents" (Nelson 1907: 170-171). "The first and all-important thing is to settle it in your minds as parents that you are going to govern your child and that it must conform to your will and desires in every respect. Never once let yourself be swayed from this needful and wise resolution" (198).

What methods were suggested by which parents might go about the challenge of conforming to their own the wills of their children? Answers to this perennial question generally stated that good parents governed through both example and punishment. Parents could train their boys and girls by setting good examples for them. Before applying corporal punishment, parents should appeal to the child's love for them and to the sense of reason present even in the young. Only when such methods failed was the rod to be applied. Early writers did not endorse all forms of physical punishment. Cuffing, slapping, ear-pulling, and "spanking" were all forbidden, and "the size of the child and its disposition" were the criteria which determined the size of the instrument of punishment (200-204).

A good deal of the advice offered by early Church of God writers followed the conventional wisdom of the conservative Protestant culture of its day. But to harsh words about governing and wills in subjection must be added other, kinder words. Our foremothers and forefathers did not always think of their children as miniature adults with whom they were locked in a perpetual contest. Allie C. Fisher, Bessie L. Byrum and, of course, Elsie Egermeier each understood that the way into any heart, but perhaps especially the hearts of children, is through stories.

Egermeier, whose *Bible Story Book* is the all-time best-seller among Gospel Trumpet Company/Warner Press books, knew better than even some of our best students of Scripture that the Bible is a wonderful story about God in search of a people who might be his own. Even more, she seems to have known instinctively that when children are deprived of that story, they are left without the surest means of negotiating the dangerous journey called life. Thus it is her book that has become the instrument by which generations of parents have helped their children envision the world and their place in it as objects of God's care and delight.

Loving and Counseling Our Children

The idea that parents can be said to have duties to their children piques my curiosity about this whole business of how the Church of God movement has educated its children. It turns out, for example, that the movement has quite a history of publishing books of advice for adolescents and young adults. Verna Joiner published *What Teens Say* in 1962. Long before that A. T. Rowe had written *Ideals for Earnest Youth* (1927), which was preceded by Mabel

Jenny Carpenter Rutty published some of the first Gospel Trumpet Company books that addressed the needs and concerns of young women and men. These books offered readers guides to manners and morals as well as theological and religious instruction.

Hale's *Beautiful Girlhood* (1922) and D. O. Teasley's, *Everyday Do's and Don'ts, or, The Art of Good Manners* (1918). But the real spring from which this stream of literature flowed was the pen of Jenny C. Rutty.

The first of Rutty's two books, *Letters of Love and Counsel to Our Girls*, was written while the Gospel Trumpet Company was still located in Grand Junction, Michigan. Rutty, born in 1856, had joined the Company as a worker there. After the publishing work relocated in Moundsville, West Virginia, she published a companion volume, *Mothers' Counsel to Their Sons*. Together these books comprise over 750 pages of advice on matters spiritual, physical, moral, domestic, and economic. You might say that Jenny Rutty was a kind of early Church of God "Dear Abby," especially because she used a letter format to structure the chapters of her book written to girls.

What kinds of subjects did Jenny Rutty discuss? Roughly one-third of each book (the book for boys, incidentally, is about 100 pages longer than the one for girls) treats religious matters. These sections resemble small catechisms in that they are straightforward doctrinal presentations. We find chapters on "Conviction," "Repentance and Conversion," "The Baptism of the Holy Ghost," "Divine Healing," and "The Church of God." In her book for girls the last chapter is arranged in the exact style of many catechisms: question followed by answer and biblical text. Her discussions of these subjects faithfully reproduce what was appearing in the *Gospel Trumpet* articles of this period. We would be surprised if that were not the case, I imagine.

When we turn to what might be called the "manners and morals" sections of these books a few of her ideas might indeed surprise us. The way she handles matters like dancing, tobacco, temperance, and "secret sins" is pretty much in keeping with late nineteenth century rural American values. I was struck by her rural framework as I read through her list of acceptable forms of recreation—walking, hiking, bicycle-riding—activities one may do in the country. Few of these would work well in 1900 New York City, and she seems to have taken no thought of what urban people might do for entertainment. That rural mind-set commonly existed among Protestants of Jenny Rutty's day.

Her attitude toward "novel-reading" is disappointing but also predictable. She thought it was frivolous and corrupted the mind. It filled the heads of young women and men with wrong ideas about love and romance (romance being the objectionable notion) and generally softened their brains. The target of her criticism leads me to think that she had in mind the dime novel and other predecessors of our contemporary paperback romances. But her blanket rejection ("touch not, read not") of all novels prohibits Dickens and Dostoyevsky along with dimestore pulp stories.

Disappointment, however, turns to surprise when we encounter her attitudes toward business and marriage. Work, according to

Jenny Rutty, was virtuous and something in which all men and some women ought to be engaged. But why work? Because it is honorable; "labor assists toward honor." She went out of her way to criticize those who labor only for economic gain, and Rutty especially attacked those who lived on investments: "We will class them as butterflies—they sip the nectar from every bud and flower, and give nothing in return" (1899: 263). She concluded by saying, "Those who are rich are to be willing to distribute, ready for every good work; so their riches would not long remain to them" (262). About Rutty's attitude toward business, labor, and wealth there hangs the scent of the same populist reform that carried William Jennings Bryan to a presidential nomination in 1896.

Perhaps even more surprising than Rutty's economic values are her ideas about marriage; she considered it a vocation. God called some to marriage but others to singleness: "We must not forget that this life [marriage] is for those whom God shall choose to call to it, for his glory and our individual good, and that there is also a life of holy service to God, where this relation, while held in honor and highest esteem, is freely yielded to the will of God, that he might have an undivided service" (262). Rutty found plenty of biblical support for a life of "holy virginity," as she called it.

Jenny Carpenter Rutty's books demonstrate enough diversity of thought that we cannot predict what she always might say. Her ideas reveal some interesting twists and turns of mind that make it impossible for us to stereotype her. When we bother to find out more than the most general and frequently stated ideas and commitments of the early leaders of the Church of God, we find a considerable diversity among them as a group, and a stimulating complexity within them as individuals. That discovery is worth remembering.

At least one other point should be remembered about Jenny Rutty and the literary genre her books represent. They were written out of the assumption that the church has a deep stake in the lives of the children. That stake extended beyond their spiritual welfare to include all aspects of their existence. "Moral and Spiritual values," to borrow a contemporary phrase, were understood quite broadly. The existence of books such as those written by Jenny C. Rutty indicates a profound interest and sense of responsibility by the church for the kind of people—the character—their children were becoming. That, too, is worth remembering.

On the Instruction of the Church's Youth

These days one reads a considerable amount of comment critical of young people. If one believes this comment, young people neither vote, even in presidential elections, nor say "thank you." They are materialistic and self-absorbed. Television has trained them to think of the world as made for their entertainment. When the entertainment fails and there is nothing to do, young people apply that universal condemnation, "This is boring" (variant—"I'm bored"), never considering that boredom may be a condition internal rather than external to the bored.

Some of this criticism of youth may hit the mark. But we should take care to remember that the young people who are the targets of such comment did not enter the world encumbered with the values for which adults now soundly castigate them. In our harsh judgments we ought to pause long enough to ask ourselves from whom these young people acquired their notions about good, evil, and the purpose of life. I suspect that young people have learned by watching their elders attach great importance to some things and less to others. What have young people learned to prize by watching us and observing what we prize?

It is altogether appropriate for the church to ask this question of itself. Equally appropriate is the church's intention to morally form its children and youth. That is, after all, part of the task of making disciples. We might give this question a more readily apparent historical twist and inquire into some of the church's earlier efforts at the moral formation of its young.

What was the church saying to its youth during those years of rebellion and restlessness, the infamous 1960s? A Sunday school lesson, written for October 12, 1969, asked learners to consider who might be a true prophet and the nature of prophecy (Youth II 1969: 18-20). The lesson also asked the provocative question, "Does God want to be popular?" The implicit answer to such a question challenges teen-agers at the center of their psyches. Young people measure themselves against the thoughts and judgments of their peers; of course they desire to fit into the majority. But the lesson on that October Sunday asked thousands of Church of God youth to consider the possibility that God is not interested in popularity. Of course, a God out of step with the majority culture should be served by a counter-cultural church.

The lesson went on to encourage young people to consider what it might mean to be a prophet in their own time. Might a modern-day prophet organize a protest or an appeal for a condemned man who could not afford an elaborate and expensive trial defense? Would a prophet stand with a welfare family whose continued attendance at church threatened to cause other, more prominent, families to leave? Basic to prophetism are the matters of justice and righteousness. The lesson of October 12, 1969, wanted young people to see the crucial importance of those two virtues for the people of God—even though they might make youth something of a cultural oddity.

In a real sense, the idea of "youth" as a period of life between childhood and adulthood was invented during the years immediately following World War II. It was in those years that the "youth culture" was created, and para-church organizations like Youth for Christ gathered great momentum.

During this era Robert Reardon, then assistant to the president at Anderson College, wrote a series of lessons for older youth entitled "Making Our Community More Christian." As the meditation for the lesson for September 11, Reardon used Washington Gladden's famous hymn text, "O Master Let Me Walk with Thee." "The church," said Reardon, "must justify its presence in any community." This justification comes through several imperatives. The church must care (a) about human suffering, (b) that the truth be known, (c) that the church be the community's conscience, (d) how community differences are settled, and (e) that Christ's kingdom would come to the heart of each member of the community (*Senior Youth* 1949: 83-88).

Reardon attempted to teach young people to think of the church as a compassionate, active body of believers. The church did not exist, in this view, to care for its members as much as to see to it that its members cared for their community. He appealed to the altruism of youth in an effort to help them understand that the business of Christian people is to give of themselves.

Thirty years earlier, in 1919, the Church of God movement did not publish quarterly material for Sunday school. But it did provide for the instruction of youth in the pages of the *Gospel Trumpet*. The paper published the regular feature "Our Young People." This column treated a wide variety of topics: the seductions of "artful women," the means by which young people attract attention to themselves, and "duty." The July 3 issue of the *Trumpet* reported on the young people's meetings at the recently concluded camp meeting in Anderson. B. F. Timmons addressed one session on the topic "How to Fill Our Place in the Body of Christ." Bertha Downing spoke on the importance of having a purpose in life, of taking care to obey God, and a willingness to shoulder responsibility (*G.T.* 1919: 18-19). As in 1969 and 1949, Church of God youth of 1919 were taught to think of the church as an entity in which one exercised his or her gifts. It was a place of ministry. The Christian life was, correlatively, thought to be a life of service. In other words, the church's older generation taught young people to serve.

If, indeed, the church's young people learned to serve and learned to think of the church as the primary arena of this service, it is because their older brothers and sisters and their parents taught them to think in such categories. They taught their younger brothers and sisters by precept and by example. The adults of former generations—our parents and grandparents—taught such a conception of the church because they believed and practiced it. Of course, the question then begs to be answered, "What sort of church, and what sort of conception of the Christian life are *we* teaching the young people of whom we are often so harshly and unfairly critical?

Church-Centered Families

At one time or another in their histories, most of the colleges owned by the Church of God governed the dating practices and even the marriages of their students. They needed the permission of the college before getting married and often just to have a date. Contemporary students who learn that Anderson, Mid-America,

Warner Pacific, and Gardner all once had such rules are initially amused. How strange to think that a college ever would believe that it had the responsibility to permit or deny its students something as personal, as private, as marriage! The students' initial amusement sometimes turns to indignation, if not moral outrage. How dare anyone tell me what I can or cannot do or be?

The technical phrase that authorized the colleges' belief that they ought to make judgments about matters like dating and marriage is called *in loco parentis*, Latin for "the parent in this locale." Under this idea, colleges assume the role of parent in matters where parental judgment seems warranted by the circumstances. I would like to think that the idea of *in loco parentis* had its origin in the movement's and the colleges' conception of what it means to be the church. So far as I know, early Church of God people did not request permission for marriage from the church. But guidance and advice both were offered. And the idea of a calling to singleness also appeared in early Church of God writing.

The point here is that there once was a time when our forefathers and foremothers thought that the church had something to say about who gets married, who does not, and for what reasons. The church may not have had much to offer on this matter, but it was believed to have something to say. The presence of such a belief would suggest that Church of God people have not thought that marriage is simply an agreement between two individuals who alone decide whether they could, and should, be married. If only in minor ways, it seems that we once thought that marriage, and by extension families, are centered in the church.

The church not only supports families, sometimes it separates them. Sometimes it calls daughters and sons to the ministry. Sometimes it sends grandchildren to a mission halfway around the world. Sometimes the church becomes a bone of contention between spouses. Read the history of the Church of God and you will discover scores of men and women for whom the church was more important than family. The church was their primary relationship. The church claimed them for God and became an instrumental cause in the long-term separation of families.

All this means that a danger lurks in our desire for "family-centered churches." The danger lies not so much in our conception of the family as in our idea about the church. The idea of the church in the phrase "family-centered church" is dangerous because that way of stating the relationship assumes that the church exists to prop up the family that is everywhere under attack. Support for the family then becomes but one more of the goods and services that are assumed to be available at the church. This assumption, perhaps harmless in itself, only increases the dangerous tendency already loose among us to think of the church as some kind of spiritual shopping center. From such shopping centers consumers feel free to choose whatever religious products are available. We often call these products "programs" or "ministries" directed to people's "needs." (Very early in our marriage, my mother-in-law warned my wife and me about confusing our "needer" with our "wanter." It was good advice then and now, and deserves to be extended far beyond the realm of marriage). Of course judgments about what in the church is worthwhile are retained by the shopper. After all, the customer is always right. Consumerist morality menaces the very life of the church.

There is another way of relating families and churches. We might think of church-centered families. In this case we are talking about our willingness to submit to the church's judgment questions like these: Should I marry? Should I marry _____? Should we have children? Where should we live? What is my vocation? Can the congregation afford my move to another location for the sake of my career?

Such a suggestion appears outrageous. And we begin to understand the outrage of the Church of God college students I mentioned at the beginning of this essay. *They* think it outrageous of a college to intrude itself in such private matters as marriage. That we think it outrageous of a church to intrude itself into such matters may very well indicate the depths of our individualism and consumerist notions of the church. That may be one of the reasons we prefer "family-centered churches" to church-centered families.

Timefulness (5)

Time in a Bottle

A few years ago a man appeared in my office door asking permission to use the Archives of the Church of God. He wanted to photocopy entire volumes of the *Gospel Trumpet*. He was interested only in the earliest volumes of the paper and certainly nothing after 1910. This man reproduces and binds his photocopies as new volumes of the *Trumpet* and makes them available to the movement of which he is a part. If I described this movement by some of its commitments—no neckties for men, no make-up for women, and refraining from the use of medicine or physicians—many might recognize them as once having been part of the Church of God movement. They would describe themselves as the Church of God movement period, and they call the "Anderson movement" what most of the rest of us think of as the Church of God.

A small group of these people once visited the Archives. They wanted to see some of the memorabilia housed in its reading room. D. S. Warner's personal belongings and his rocker proved to be of much greater interest than either E. E. Byrum's desk or the brick from the movement's first church building. We sang some songs together and enjoyed a lively conversation. One of the group asked me whether anyone at Anderson University taught a course in Church of God history and doctrine. I told them that I did, and then

I added these words, "But you must understand that when I teach that course, I do not teach it as if doctrine stopped in 1909." The people with whom I sang and talked on that autumn afternoon love God with all their hearts. My intention is not to poke fun at them or impugn their integrity and faith in any way. But we do disagree on some matters of considerable importance. At bottom, this disagreement is over whether or not time can be stopped, whether it can be placed in a bottle and corked tight.

Students in my courses on the history of the Church of God often want to write papers in which they plan to demonstrate that the movement has changed. Somehow they infer that change always is sinister. They believe that D. S. Warner would be shocked by what he would see, were he suddenly to return from the dead. I remind my students that virtually any nineteenth century person would be shocked by the developments of the last hundred years. But then, people of the late eighteenth century would have been shocked, most likely, by the society of Warner's day. Time, that ever-rolling stream, will overflow the largest of bottles; it will not be stopped up.

Most of us may not view time from the extreme perspective of those visitors to the Archives two years ago, but we often find other ways to make things stop, so to speak. If something can be made to stop it will never change. I am convinced that a deep need for certainty prompts us to seek or create these unchangeable forms. This quest for certainty prompts our church life in directions that will, if followed too far, lead us to place our trust where it does not properly belong.

The history of the Church of God movement bears the scars of many a controversy where this quest for certainty erupted into open conflicts. I have written about many of these controversies. The case often seems to be that our controversies have emerged as someone or some group among us has sought certainty where it could not be found. When people of the movement struggled with each other over matters of apparel or entertainment, they looked to found certainty on homogeneous appearance or behavior. Thus they could be certain of their beliefs because the saints all looked alike or acted in the same ways. Others have wanted to rest their certainty on doctrinal homogeneity; if we all believe the same things, then we will be certain. Of course, such attitudes are what lead people to trust in creeds. Despite our long opposition to creeds, the desire for certainty has tempted us here, too—on more than one occasion. Still others have thought that the movement's confident facing of its future, if not its certainty, rests in some version of its polity, as if the right form of organization was a panacea either for the movement or a congregation. Certainty does not lie in this reductionism, either.

The church is a storied people. Ultimately this conviction about the church underlies my interest in the stories of the men and women who have been a part of the Church of God movement. Occasionally we must step back from the stories themselves and ask an important question about the attitude with which we can appropriately hold and tell the stories we treasure. We would be a faithless people were we to forget those stories. We would be equally faithless were we to seek certainty in them. That would be to think that time and truth could be bottled. Not even God thought to bottle time and truth. Truth, the Logos, came in the form of a baby and pitched his tabernacle among us.

The Marion Three

In the June 9, 1898 issue of the *Gospel Trumpet* bold headlines screamed the news that three of the saints had been charged with murder. Late in May, Mrs. Sarah Johnson of Marion, Indiana, had died from complications of childbirth. Mrs. Johnson had refused the medicine prescribed by her attending physician. Her husband and two Church of God gospel workers supported Sarah in her decision. So it was that a few days after her death, the Grant County sheriff arrested them on the charge of murder. The next several issues of the *Trumpet* carried news of the affair, and those issues shed considerable light on some of the movement's early commitments.

After Sarah Johnson delivered their baby, her husband, William, had cared for her the best he could. Sarah Achor also offered her care when she visited Mrs. Johnson during her "confinement." Mrs. Achor's husband, George, telephoned often, voicing over the phone his prayers for the stricken woman. Because the Johnsons believed in the doctrine of divine healing, they followed the famous passage in James 5 and called for the elders to come, anoint, and pray for Sarah. George and Sarah Achor answered that call. Ironically, George Achor had practiced medicine and even lectured on medical subjects for some twelve years prior to being called into the ministry. Only a few months prior to the incident he had lectured on anatomy. But Achor had used none of his medical expertise in caring for Mrs. Johnson, and for that he was charged with murder along with his wife and William Johnson.

The editorial staff of the *Gospel Trumpet* interpreted the actions of the citizens of Marion toward the Achors and William Johnson as persecution. The saints' accusers were viewed as enemies of Christianity. They made their false accusations out of a sectarian spirit that was, in the *Trumpet's* words, prejudiced against the truth.

The *Gospel Trumpet* followed the court case through the summer and early fall of 1898. People from the editorial staff visited the three saints incarcerated in the Grant County jail and reported on the good spirit they found there. The paper carried descriptions of praying and singing in jail that surely reminded readers of the first century hymn-sing at Philippi. Later in the summer the county prosecutor dropped the murder charges and referred the case to the grand jury, which returned an indictment of involuntary manslaughter. The Achors and Johnson then were released on bail pending their trial that September.

After their release, the Achors published their testimony of God's goodness to them during their imprisonment. From their perspective their stay in jail "was a means of very great spiritual advancement in the community as well as their own lives (*G.T.* 1898: 6). The paper predicted that the Achors' trial would be the means by which God would vindicate the doctrine of divine healing.

The trial itself got underway in late September and lasted for five days. The state called some thirty witnesses while the defense called none. The physician who had attended Mrs. Johnson testified that she had stopped taking her prescription because it was only making her sicker. He concluded that since her condition was worsening she had acted wisely in discontinuing the medicine. After all the evidence was in, the trial ended in a hung jury and the charges were dropped.

Sarah and George Achor, early Church of God evangelists and Gospel workers in Indiana. George Achor left a medical career to pursue the ministry of evangelist and revivalist. Along with his wife and Mr. William Johnson, Achor was arraigned by a Grant County (Indiana) court on charges connected with the death of Johnson's wife, who died of complications associated with childbirth. All three were subsequently tried, but none was convicted of any wrongdoing.

On one view, this is a story about the doctrine of divine healing. That is certainly how Editor E. E. Byrum interpreted the whole affair. The *Trumpet* articles that described the plight of the Achors and William Johnson also carried broad charges against the medical community. Byrum wanted to know why it was that physicians were not charged with manslaughter whenever one of their patients died. Why was it always divine healing that came under attack? The questions that Byrum repeatedly raised in his articles indicate that he saw the accusations against this trio as a form of persecution directed at those who trusted God for healing.

On another view, the story of the "Marion Three" illustrates a truth larger than the doctrine of divine healing. Sarah and William Johnson and George and Sarah Achor all were prepared to trust God in the matter, thereby relinquishing the stubborn human insistence that our lives are our own. Their act of giving their lives over to God, whether on a sickbed or in a jail cell, reminds us how strange the church appears to a world that refuses to acknowledge God.

Israel in Canaan, the church spreading out in the Roman Empire, or three saints praying for a sick and dying woman in Marion, Indiana, appear rather strange according to the judgment of this world. The Church of God movement understood the fact that "the world" judged it strange in the summer of 1898, and that judgment they seem to have accepted. They did not relish the trouble it brought them. But on the other hand, they were prepared to endure that trouble because the saints knew that it was the consequence of their stubborn allegiance to God. In the matter of serving God and the world, they knew they could not have it both ways. The people of God never can.

Constancy

The students in my courses on the history of the Church of God history inevitably find themselves pondering some of the controversies in the movement. Controversies do not simply happen; they do not set themselves in motion. People cause controversies, and in the church we hope that these people are well-intentioned folk with honest differences. I suppose the church also includes contentious souls who love to argue; but the people who have been part of the movement's controversies generally have not been that sort.

My students made two observations about some of our most controversial moments: the conflicts that swirled around Anderson College from 1929 to 1934. My students initially observed that, despite deep division, these controversies produced no large-scale enduring schisms. Even though the Church of God ministers were almost evenly divided on the question of John Morrison's 1934 ratification (which really was a movement-wide referendum on the kind of curriculum the college would have), we did not divide after the vote was announced. Schisms often have occurred where sentiments were not nearly as deep and evenly divided.

The students in my course also often observe the virtue of constancy in the people who were so deeply embroiled in these controversies. Constancy is the quality of our character that enables us to change and adapt to change while we keep our eyes fixed on the same goal. Christians of the ancient world described the church as a ship—the ark of salvation. We might extend that metaphor and think of the church as a ship on a voyage. Constancy is the ability of those on board this ship to keep at it. Constancy is the skill employed by "travelers in the midst of the vicissitudes of the journey [who] learn to trust one another when the going gets rough" (Hauerwas and William 1989: 64).

Consider all those people in the history of the Church of God who, when the going got rough in one controversy or another, refused to jump ship and who also resisted the temptation to remain on board only to complain. None of the first four editors of the Gospel Trumpet voluntarily retired from that assignment. D. S. Warner died while in office, so we may focus on the other three—E. E. Byrum, F. G. Smith, and C. E. Brown—for each of whom the going got rough. But none of them left the movement, nor did they undermine their successors.

Russell and Bessie Byrum suffered through his heresy trial and rejoiced when he was acquitted; the going had gotten rough. After his exoneration Russell took two extraordinary actions. He resigned the position he loved and the vocation to which he was called rather than damage the institution he served, and, in the dawn of his prime, he changed careers without public recrimination against the church. In all this turmoil Bessie might have turned her back on the church, but she didn't. She gave the balance of her long life to the church's educational ministry. All of these people, and many, many others in the movement's history, by such attitudes and actions display the virtue of constancy.

"Constancy requires a particular kind of change. If we are to be true to the quest, to keep a demanding goal before ourselves, we must be people who are ready to be surprised, ready to forgive and be forgiven" (64). This idea calls to mind the maneuver of sailing vessels called "tacking." When the ship's home port lays on a course that requires its crew to sail into the wind, they cannot reach their goal except by sailing back and forth oblique to the wind. Were you to measure the ship's course by reference to its prow during any one of these tacks, you would conclude that the ship no longer was sailing toward its goal. But each tack—or change— must be measured against the larger view; does it enable us to reach the voyage's goal? Not all our tacks are perfect—which means that we will need to admit our failings and mistakes in order to be forgiven and to forgive.

This calls to mind a story about F. G. Smith. A young minister, troubled by the differences between the first and second editions of Smith's *The Revelation Explained*, is reported to have asked Smith how he could have changed his views. According to the story, Smith is said to have replied, "Young man, give me credit for having thought about *something* during the last twenty-five years." Constancy—the willingness to be surprised by change while on course toward home port.

Toward the end of his tenure at Anderson College, John Morrison, like Smith a man who had been often in the midst of controversy, enjoyed quoting Abraham Lincoln's observation that since the worst of us have so much good, and the best of us so much bad, "the best of us cannot afford to despise the rest of us." Constancy—the readiness to forgive and be forgiven. Constancy is that quality to which we can point in the saints, "where we see, over time, a people being true to their originating *telos* [ultimate destiny], still on the way to the goal, through twists and turns, eyes still fixed on the quest—friendship with God in Christ."[1]

True Within My Heart

The late John W. V. Smith observed that early Church of God writers frequently used the word "Bible" as an adjective. Thus they wrote about *Bible* proofs, *Bible* salvation, *Bible* ordinances, *Bible* truth (1980: 84). One of C. W. Naylor's songs teaches us to promise that we will worship God "in the Bible way, as the evening light doth shine." "Bible" was the all-important adjective in that it legitimated whatever followed; if any position could not be verified from the Bible, it was not to be believed.

We must hasten to say, however, that early Church of God folk did not stop once the Bible had been read and believed. Trace our theological heritage back from Warner through the Holiness Movement to John and Charles Wesley, from the Wesleys through Zinzendorf and A. H. Franke to Philip J. Spener and Johannes Arndt and you will discover the movement's historical and theological connections with the seventeenth century Pietists. Masters of the devotional life populate this long line of earnest Christians, men and women driven by one all-important question: "How are the insights of the Bible to be applied to everyday life?" (Stoeffler 1971:20).

Certainly Christians ought to believe the Bible. But more than a source of dogma, the Bible was (and is) a book to be *lived*. Thus we used to sing songs about how the Bible's truths were "proved" in our hearts. As one song put it, " 'Tis Better Felt than Told"; first-hand experience surpasses second-hand knowledge.

We have been a people of the Bible, to be sure. But we have not been people of the Word only. In 1925, C. W. Naylor published another in a series of devotional books that he wrote while bedfast with an injury he had suffered in 1910. In this volume *God's Will and How to Know It*, Naylor treated topics of great importance to men and women hungering for a closer walk with God. One of the topics discussed at length by Naylor was how God reveals his will.

Given the way we talked about "Bible" truths in 1925, one might expect Naylor to say that God reveals his will in Scripture, period. But Naylor knew experientially that the devotional life prospered in a subtle and delicately balanced harmony of Word and Spirit. God revealed his will in many ways, said Naylor. Human reason, the natural order, and "human instrumentality" all were divinely-appointed means for communicating God's will to the seeker. But the means that most intrigued Naylor was the way God worked through the Holy Spirit to communicate his will to human beings.

Echoing Jesus' promise that the Spirit would guide us into all truth (and how very many of the movement's preachers and writers laid hold of that same text), Naylor said that the Spirit revealed

Although perhaps best known as a poet and songwriter, Charles W. Naylor (1874-1950) authored several devotional books, including *The Secret of a Singing Heart, Winning A Crown, Heart Talks,* and *When Adversity Comes.*

truth gradually and increasingly. Earthly life could not contain the knowledge ultimately available through the Spirit. Only in the next life would we "know even as we are known" (50).

Naylor of course insisted that the Spirit illuminated the lives of those who had been born again. Regeneration, the new birth, inaugurated a personal relationship between the soul and God. The significance of the word "personal" does not lie in the sense of private—as in a personal possession. Rather, the meaning here is that the relationship begun in the new birth is one between two persons, the human soul and the Divine Being. The knowledge transmitted in that bond is of the mysterious nature that always characterizes the experiential knowledge of one person with another. This experiential knowing is the locus of the soul's assurance of salvation. Deeply personal and resting in the ongoing experience of life in the Spirit, this knowledge is not the objective "knowledge that . . ." It is the subjective, intimate friendship of our souls with the Divine Spirit.

So early Church of God writers read and believed the Bible. They needed no philosophical or theological arguments to prove the Bible was authoritative. They simply took it to be so. Why? Because the Bible opened the way to real religion in the soul. As an early Church of God gospel song I frequently quote put it:

I have read within the Bible
what His favor will impart.
And, oh glory! I have proved it.
Now 'tis true within my heart.

Daring Developments

The poster which advertised the 1919 camp meeting at
Anderson announced many features of that meeting. Daily services
began at 10:30 each morning, 2:15 in the afternoon and 8:00 at
night. Lunches and refreshments could be procured on the campground. Lodging could be secured for two dollars for the week or
forty cents a night; people who brought their own bedding received
a twenty-five percent discount.

Preachers addressed the topics of unity, salvation, prophecy,
purity of heart and divine healing. The poster also announced that
on June 17 Assistant Surgeon W. F. King of the U.S. Public Health
Service would speak at the 2:15 service, "in the interests of the
campaign against venereal disease."

The presence of a Public Health Service physician speaking in
an official capacity to a Church of God camp meeting crowd on the
topic of venereal disease is extremely interesting. For one thing,
the delicate nature of the topic is one that I had thought would not
be discussed in polite conversation, let alone at a church meeting.
Some of those responsible for the organization of the meeting obviously thought that this was a private matter of such public significance that camp meeting crowds needed to hear about it. Perhaps
Assistant Surgeon King hoped to gain the support of Christian people for the national campaign to combat syphilis and gonorrhea.
Whatever King's motives, the simple fact that he came to Anderson
Camp Meeting to address this subject publicly says something
about the people who made room for him on the program.

Another interesting aspect of King's visit to the camp meeting of
1919 is that he was a physician talking to a group of people who
did not think much of doctors. In those years the back page of the
Gospel Trumpet still carried a feature called "Divine Healing."
There people could read the testimonies of men and women who
were happy to say that they had long ago given up on doctors and

medicines, and trusting God completely for the healing of their bodies. In 1919 many Church of God people neither trusted nor liked physicians. Yet they entertained a doctor on the camp meeting platform that year. This event seems to indicate something of the change that was beginning in our attitude toward doctors and medicine. Several elements in this change help us to understand it.

Part of the process of change in the movement's ideas about physicians and medicine are the phenomenal developments in the practice of medicine since 1880. Many Americans, and not only Church of God people, did not trust doctors in the nineteenth century, and with good reason. When the Church of God movement came into being, the practice of medicine was just that—practice, and rudimentary at that. Even Dr. W. W. Mayo, whose sons founded the famous medical clinic in Rochester, Minnesota, once was reduced to asking one of his young sons to administer anesthesia to a surgery patient after the original "anesthesiologist" fainted at the sight of blood. The boy stood on overturned an cracker box in order to reach the patient.

Rural Americans observed that a number of sick people seemed to become even sicker after seeing a doctor. As medical schools improved and the medical profession came under standardization and regulation, however, these conditions improved. By 1919, the practice of medicine had changed remarkably from conditions of only thirty-five or forty years earlier. Doctors could do much more for their patients, and even greater possibilities awaited discovery in the following two decades. Think, for example, of how the discovery and use of penicillin in 1942 virtually eliminated the threat of an infection as deadly as pneumonia. But even in 1919 we were beginning to realize that doctors could really help people.

Another element that contributed to the change that allowed W. F. King to address the 1919 camp meeting was a change in the movement's attitude toward divine healing. Our attitude changed, in part, because our theology of healing could not explain some of the cases among us where no physical healing occurred. We now recall the well-known examples of the tragic deaths of Clarence and Nora Hunter's infant daughters and the debilitating suffering of C. W. Naylor. Surely other people, less widely known, endured similar tragedies, and compassionate souls in their local fellowships began re-thinking the movement's theology of healing. Over time our theological development came to regard the use of physicians and medicines as wholly within the circle of God's loving care. Thus even without the great improvements in health care and medicine, developments internal to the Church of God movement pushed us to change our ideas and our teaching on divine healing. These changes surely were part of the reason that we gave Assistant Surgeon King the opportunity to speak.

What is there to be learned from this apparently commonplace event in Anderson in 1919? One lesson is to observe the movement's theological flexibility and capacity for doctrinal development. The 1919 camp meeting included healing services where the sick and afflicted were anointed and for whom the elders prayed. The fact that a doctor was on the program did not alter that practice. Living church doctrine must have this kind of continuity *and* the capacity for growth and development demonstrated by our forefathers and foremothers.

Second, the camp meeting crowd dared to entertain a subject that often went ignored by decent folk—venereal disease. Their posters even announced that they intended to discuss the matter. And why not? The disease was important, and the church ought to be the kind of people who talk about important matters.

AIDS is important, and that may be the understatement of the twentieth century. We know that AIDS is far more than a sexually transmitted disease. It is a scourge that might strike those who receive blood transfusions or organ transplants, to name but two ways people can contract this terrible illness. Perhaps the program for some contemporary camp meeting should announce that some respected national authority on AIDS will be addressing the Wednesday afternoon service.

Setting Type All Day

Use a phrase like "the early days of the Church of God movement," and most of us will recall the "great events" of that era. We likely will first remember the celebrated October day at Beaver Dam, Indiana, where D. S. Warner took his stand against all humanly devised forms of church organization. Some of us might recall Warner's equally dramatic protest-resignation from the Indiana State Holiness Association the previous spring. Others of us probably would call to mind Benjamin Elliott's inaugural missionary journey into Mexico. The history of the movement is full of such events; many others could be suggested.

The history of any religious movement, the Church of God included, narrates much, much more than "great events." Movements and congregations are sustained and nourished by day-to-day activities undertaken by women and men who will never be included in books with titles like *Who Was Who In American Religious History.* That such books do not include these people has nothing to do, of course, with the significance of their contributions. Recently I read Rhoda Keagy Byrum's journal for 1888, and that experience forcefully struck home again the point that the body of Christ has many members who are called to many different tasks—all of which nurture the body.

Rhoda Keagy (d. 1907) and Celia Kilpatrick (d. 1888) together comprised the sum total of the *Gospel Trumpet* clerical staff in the year 1888. Enoch Byrum, the paper's publisher, had been at his post for less than two years. As the new year opened, Editor D. S Warner and his company of singers and gospel workers were off on an evangelistic tour. We may not be entirely justified in referring to the little band of Grand Junction workers as a skeleton crew, but that could not have been very far from the truth.

Byrum gave Rhoda a blank journal volume for 1888 in which she faithfully entered the small band's assignments and activities. This open window on the Trumpet family's life gives us a wonderful picture of its daily work and occasional recreation. It reveals something of the personalities and struggles of some of the people who were part of the movement's life in those years. From Rhoda's entries we glimpse the boisterous personality of Anna Speck, a young woman undergoing her own crisis of faith. Yet Anna once set the young women in a Saints' meeting to giggling, provoking enough laughter to cause people to tip over rocking chairs. Those of us whose vision of the movement's early days was a sober one will be surprised to learn that Anna, Rhoda, and four other young women once spent most of an afternoon trying to throw each other onto one of the Trumpet family beds.

The hilarity of a rowdy afternoon only infrequently interrupted the days of close, repetitive, and often tedious labor associated with the publishing work. Rhoda filled her journal with entries such as: [March 28] "I set type all day"; [March 29] "Celia and I finished setting the type for the last side of April first" [edition of the *Gospel Trumpet*]; [March 30] "We printed this morning. . . we folded the papers and rapped [*sic*] some"; [March 31] "I gathered song books up till half past 2 o'clock." Except Sundays, nearly every day of the week carries an entry that refers to some task connected with the *Trumpet*. Somebody, usually Rhoda, was always setting type or building forms to hold it. When not typesetting, folding, or wrapping, Rhoda often proofread galley pages of new publications.

The *Trumpet* family employed some of its time in tasks necessary for their physical well-being. Caring for their material needs meant that workers could not devote all their time to type racks or presses. Thus they spent time preparing their own meals and sewing much of their own clothing. Rhoda also refers to spending some of her evenings tearing rags for rugs. But the *Trumpet* family also took time for simple pleasures like taking walks in the woods outside Grand Junction, playing such games as "blind-fold" and "wolf", and popping corn during a long, quiet evening.

Celia Kilpatrick's illness runs like a thread through Rhoda's journal. These two young women were sisters in Christ, and they were friends bound together in a common vocation. Early in her journal Rhoda began referring to Celia's illness. Some times she became so ill as to become delirious. But sickness did not prevent Celia's marriage to Enoch Byrum in March. Her condition worsened, however, and Rhoda feared for her friend's life. As she wrote in her elegant and heartfelt simplicity: [Apr. 2] "Oh! I felt so bad, I—O dear! I could scarcely work. Celia feels quite bad today. . ."; [Apr. 6] "Celia does not seem to get any better"; [Dec. 10] "Poor Celia! she will soon be done with this world." Celia Kilpatrick Byrum died the following day, as Rhoda said, "Four years to-day since I came to the Trumpet office, & the February after, Dear Celia came, and we have been together nearly ever since then."

Rhoda's journal concludes with the close of 1888, so we do not have access to her ideas and emotions in the first months of 1889. It was then that Enoch Byrum's thoughts and affection turned

Early Gospel Trumpet Company workers at Grand Junction, Michigan. Standing in the middle (behind the seated D. S. Warner and E. E. Byrum) are Rhoda Keagy and Celia Kilpatrick, both of whom eventually married Byrum.

toward her. They were married in June of that year, and Rhoda and Enoch became the parents of six children before her death in 1907.

Rhoda Keagy Byrum's 1888 journal gives only a tantalizingly brief look into her life as well as those of her friends. It is dangerous to attempt a complete portrait of those lives from one rather slender source. Nevertheless, I will hazard one small conclusion about the characters of Rhoda and Celia, and that is to say that both of these women displayed an admirable stability.

Rhoda and Celia were, of course, friends, and philosophers throughout the centuries have said that friendships will not endure between people who are inconstant. The constancy that kept these two women at their daily *Trumpet* chores and which undergirded their friendship "turns out to be possible only if we are able through our lives to point to a source outside our lives that makes it possible. Or, put more directly, the constancy of our character is not finally 'ours,' but is the result of a relation that would be impossible without the willingness of God to always be there" (Hauerwas 1990: 45). The constancy of Rhoda's and Celia's lives points to God. That constancy also nourishes the body of Christ with a vitality rarely matched by "great events."

Symbolic Connections

Driving east along Interstate 64 through eastern Kentucky will carry motorists into the horse country called the "Bluegrass." Well-maintained board fences divide the rolling terrain into elegantly kept farms where play horses that resemble neither in shape nor price tag the two tired draft-horses on Grandpa Strege's farm. East of Lexington, the ground begins to rise toward the Appalachians. Before reaching the mountains, however, you will arrive at Winchester, where a congregation of the Church of God movement formed in the early days of this century still worships.

Crossing the Ohio River brings a person into a region where memory is alive. I never fail to be impressed by the careful manner in which real southerners treasure the past. The building that houses the Church of God at Winchester illustrates this regional tendency to remember. On the narthex wall hang portrait photographs of every pastor to have served the congregation. There visitors will see the faces of N. S. Duncan, who once loosened a rope dividing blacks and whites at a camp meeting in northern Alabama before the turn of the century, and Carl Kardatzke, whose name is inevitably connected with Anderson University but who also pastored the Winchester church for a few months. A photo of the late Dale Whalen hangs on that wall as do photos of other well-known or colorful figures now gone—Harry L. Harp and "Jumpin' Joe" Lykins to name but two.

The Winchester church sanctuary windows, as in many churches, are dedicated to the memory of people whose lives have been important to the life of the congregation that worships there. In the south wall, at the very rear of the sanctuary, such a window memorializes Reverend and Mrs. G. M. Byrd, Charles Byrd Young, and Wendell Byrd. That last name connects the Winchester church and Anderson University. The School of Theology library formerly was named also for Wendell Byrd. Who was this man and why have people in Winchester and Anderson thought it so important to remember him by the symbolic means of a window and a library?

Wendell Byrd, AC Class of '36, was a minister of the Church of God who entered the United States Army as a chaplain during World War II. Byrd had come to Anderson College from Piqua, Ohio during the darkest days of the Great Depression. While in college he gained quite a reputation as a basketball player and captain of the squad in his senior year. He also was the president of the French Club and a member of the Student Council. His compassion for the poor and sick further distinguished him among a senior class that included such people as Boyce Blackwelder, Claire Shultz and E. E. Kardatzke. In the years following graduation Byrd served churches in Palmer and Anchorage, Alaska, and Piqua.

After serving in the South Pacific, Byrd entered the Reserve Chaplain Corps at the war's end. A few years later, after the Korean War began, Captain Byrd was recalled to active duty in November of 1950. Less than a year later, October 27, 1951, Chaplain Byrd was killed among the soldiers to whom he was ministering in Korea. In his published announcement of Byrd's death, John Kane, then alumni director at Anderson College, said that the deaths of all AC alumni killed in action seemed futile, and he noted that war had written a particularly dark story on a wonderful Christian family. Two of Wendell's nephews had been killed during World War II, as had his brother.

In 1953, when the congregation at Winchester was building a new sanctuary, some people there thought it important to remember Wendell Byrd and other members of his family. Seven years later, when the School of Theology library got its own permanent quarters, other people also thought it important to remember Chaplain Byrd and his father, a long-time Church of God pastor, and so they named the place "Byrd Library" in their memory. Today, Anderson University students walk through the east end of Nicholson

A hall in Anderson University's library memorializes Wendell Byrd (1910-1951), an alumnus of Anderson College and a minister of the Church of God. Byrd served churches in Alaska and Ohio before volunteering for duty as a military chaplain in World War II. Recalled to active duty in 1950, he was killed in Korea.

Library, "Byrd Hall," scarcely noticing the portraits of the two Byrds and probably ignorant of their stories. Similarly, people of the Winchester congregation enter the sanctuary for worship and likely do not reflect on the memory of the man and family whose name distinguishes the last window in the south wall. That everyone does not remember the story of the man behind these symbols is not important; it is only necessary that some remember, and that, from time to time they tell this story. The enduring presence of a window, or a name cast in a bronze plaque on a library wall, stand there against the day when someone will ask about the name and another will explain why we have remembered them.

Advent and Christmas are seasons rich in symbolism, even if we do not always remember that which these symbols signify. Many of us have trees in our houses, Advent wreaths and candles in our sanctuaries, and drink a beverage we call "wassail" without really knowing what we are doing or very much about that for which these symbols stand. We will also read of mysterious magi from an unknown eastern land who bring to the Christ Child gifts symbolizing his kingly and high priestly offices and the vicarious suffering and sacrifice of his death.

Symbols and symbolic places invoke our memories. There is, or ought to be, an inescapable connection between stories and symbols. We should not find it necessary to invent symbols or, having invented them, construct explanations of their presence or significance. Rather, symbols rise out of stories. They focus our attention on events and people whose lives contribute to the narrative that forms the web of moral meaning in which our lives are shaped. Without that focused memory, we are like children of the fairy tales who have lost their way in a deep and very dark wood. In our innermost beings we sense this to be true, and thus our hunger to fill our lives with new symbols and traditions. But a "new tradition" is a contradiction in terms. Better to return to the old stories and ask our fathers and mothers to tell them to us again and again.

II

Theological and Moral Essays on the Church

The "Malling" of the Church

6

That astute and oft-quoted observer of American religious life Martin Marty once wrote that the first amendment to the Federal Constitution drove the formerly state-established churches of the American colonies into the marketplace (1970: 35-39). The day the constitution became the law of the land American churches were thrown into competition with one another. No longer would they enjoy the benefits of governmental sanction; nor would tax revenues any longer find their way into church treasuries. In order to survive, American religious groups found it necessary to adapt to their new social situation and compete for attention, membership, and support.

A few religious movements flourished in the young nation's new, market-like environment. Nathan Hatch has portrayed the manner in which these popular denominations gained the allegiance of common people in nineteenth century America (1970: 35-39). Denominations such as the Methodists, Baptists, and Churches of Christ grew rapidly during the first half of the nineteenth century by aligning themselves with the populist, democratic and antiestablishment forces at work among middle and working-class Americans. One very important result of this adaptation has been a continuous support of religious institutions among working-class Americans, quite unlike the experience of their European counterparts. While the popular denominations' adaptiveness has retained working-class Americans' church loyalty, this marketplace strategy also laid the first stones of the foundation for a consumerist approach toward American church life.

After more than two centuries of development in the American religious experience, the marketplace has grown into a veritable shopping mall of spirituality. In the corridors of this mall consumers of religion may select from a large and growing array of programs and "ministries." The choices range from participating in traditional congregational life to watching religious programming on television; from joining a religious special purpose group [such as a fellowship of Christian drag racers or an association of Christian secretaries] to the now infamous individualistic religion of Sheila Larson in *Habits of the Heart*: "I believe in God. I'm not a religious fanatic. I can't remember the last time I went to church. My faith has carried me a long way. It's Sheilaism. . . . It's just try to love yourself and be gentle with yourself. You know, I guess, take care of each other" (Bellah 1985, 221). Many of the options in the American spiritual marketplace fall within the bounds of Christian theism. But anyone who walks the streets of even a medium-sized American city knows that those so inclined may choose a religious expression from a range of spiritualities where the options extend far beyond Christianity.

My purpose here is neither to discuss or lament the bewildering array of religious expressions now available to Americans. I do not intend to deliver yet another jeremiad on the moral and spiritual decline of American society. Rather, I wish to offer some thoughts on the social, political and economic forces at work in our culture that have brought us to the odd notion that religion, and even whether to "be religious," are matters about which people now choose in a manner similar to which they select a meal from a menu or purchase socks. These forces exert powerful influences on the church and its ministry. If we can understand better the context in which we work, then perhaps we will better understand ourselves and our common calling as followers of Jesus.

Beyond offering a social analysis, I want to draw on a similar situation in the history of the people Israel as a means of offering all of us a better alternative than simply acquiescing to the spirit of the age. Walter Brueggemann reminds us that biblical faith refuses to separate hope from history. If we do no more than understand our context, we will inevitably fall into the despair that grows out of the sense that we have been overwhelmed by history. On the other hand, to grasp for a hope that ignores the hard questions forced upon us by our historical context merely substitutes hype for a true hope (1987: 3). The elders of Israel also found themselves under enormous pressure to conform to their historical situation during the crucial years that marked the transition in leadership from Samuel to the establishment of the monarchy. By examining that critical period in the life of Israel, we may learn how to live more faithfully as the people of God.

1. Success, Entertainment, and Well-being: Life in the Consumer Culture

A few years ago while my sons and I were watching a baseball game on television I became interested in a particular commercial that aired between innings. This commercial seemed completely out of place in the middle of a ballgame. Rather than beer or smokeless tobacco, the commercial advertised potato chips, and "light" chips at that. In the context of a ballgame the ad seemed rather odd, for I assume that few television sports fans care whether their junk-food comes light or regular. But this commercial displayed even stronger incongruities, for its visual setting was a swimming pool in and around which were arrayed three beautiful young women clad in wet swimsuits made of a thin fabric that clung to their curvaceous bodies. The ad's scene had little if anything to do with the baseball game it sponsored, but the selling strategy had everything to do with baseball fans. I asked my adolescent sons the question running around in my own head, "What is being sold here, anyway?" They first answered, predictably enough, "potato chips." I suggested they think a little harder about what they had seen, and then one of the boys said, "Uh—women?" My sons were getting warm.

An important shift occurred in American advertising strategy shortly after the turn of the twentieth century. The dimensions of this shift help us to understand some of the profound changes which have ordered our society according to its capacity and desire to consume. Very little in American life, not even the church, escapes the influence of this ordering. What are its origins and dimensions?

In the nineteenth century people read or listened to advertisements in the expectation of being informed about the products they described. Deception was always a possibility, but the distribution of information, in some sense, nevertheless was well-nigh universally understood to be the point of advertisements. By the early 1900s, however, ad agencies had begun discussing the psychology of advertising. In the aftermath of this discussion advertisers' strategy shifted from *informing* potential consumers to creating in those consumers *feelings of well-being* associated with products appearing in ads (Lears 1983: 3-38, esp. 17-30). T. J. Jackson Lears argues that the shift in advertising did not in itself create the American consumer culture. Rather, the new advertising was part of a larger transition in the larger society. In this transition American cultural values moved from the goal of salvation and deferred reward to the goal of achieving well-being in social, psychological, and physical terms. It is this movement in cultural values that made possible the creation of a consumer culture. Lears and his associate Richard Fox argue that this shift is a crucial moment in the history of American culture, for it signifies a change from a "Protestant ethos ordered to the conception of salvation through self-denial to a therapeutic ethos stressing self-realization in this world—an ethic characterized by an almost obsessive concern with psychic and physical health defined in sweeping terms."[1]

In a particularly cogent discussion of America's moral traditions, Roger Betsworth traces what he calls the cultural narrative of well-being. He has in mind the therapeutic ethos which Fox and Lears place at the center of the consumer culture.

> In the cultural narrative of well-being, we seek self-realization, self-worth, and self-esteem. We wish to be attractive, charismatic, creative, dominant, or forceful. But we think not only about self but about our world with these images, which arise from psychotherapy. The

therapeutic attitude enters the world of work and helps us translate our experience of a bureaucratic society into personal meanings. When we speak of our marriages, families, friends, communities, and society, we talk in terms of communication, empathy, authenticity, and well being. Although most persons do not participate in therapy, still the therapeutic metaphors have become a major resource for thinking about society as well as the self.[2]

The cultural narrative of well-being trains us to evaluate our situation in terms of personal fulfillment. We come to think of that fulfillment as a birthright, if we think of it at all. More likely, Americans simply believe the notion of well-being as the goal of our actions to be part of the fabric of the universe; it is a part of our "assumed reality." Advertisers learned to create messages that prompt potential customers to associate feelings of well-being with the products being advertised. In the consumer culture, then, the unarticulated goal of our purchases becomes well-being, or one of its close relatives—pleasure, happiness, success, and the like. These become the ground and even the moral authority for economic decisions; they make us feel good.

In no other areas of the consumer culture is the narrative of well-being more deeply embedded than advertising, the mass-media, and television, in particular. In a deeply disturbing book, Neil Postman has explored television's influence on forms of public discourse in America (1985). Unlike most criticisms of television, Postman's book readily concedes television's unexcelled success as a medium of entertainment. Indeed, television is problematic precisely because of its extraordinary ability to entertain and to transform all forms of public discourse into entertainment (83-98). Under television's single eye, therefore, the generation of Americans who have grown up under its influence have come to believe in an inalienable right to be entertained. A corollary of this notion is the belief that when we are not being entertained, the problem is not in us but in the ostensible source of our amusement. These beliefs place all forms of public discourse [political debates and speeches, classroom lectures, public worship] under the expectation that they, like television, will be entertaining. The problem, of course, is that forms of public discourse are often not entertaining at all, but a good deal of plain, hard work. In the age of televised entertainment, however, we have been trained to avoid the hard work of attentiveness, critical listening, and reflection in favor of good feelings, i.e., the pleasure, which are correlative of our being entertained—and thus not bored.[3]

The therapeutic culture and its associated notions of the primacy of entertainment join forces with a consumerist morality to complete the picture I wish to paint of the enormous pressures on the church to conform to the spirit of the age. We are all familiar with this consumerist morality, and in fact our own activity as purchasers of goods and services reinforces our implicit belief in it; the consumer culture is part of the presumed world of most Americans. I dare say that most residents of our society would be equally shocked by a salesperson who attempted to persuade us that we really wanted to keep an item that we had just entered the store to return. As customers, i.e., consumers, we know that we are "always right." That is to say, our purchasing choices are always correct. Who is to tell us what we should or should not purchase? Certainly not the retailer. The customer's choices are, by definition, always right, and from them there is no appeal. The notions that our choices are ours alone, that we are free to choose as we will, and that the unstated but real goal of our choices is our well-being are the cornerstones of American consumerist morality.

The consumerist, or market, morality penetrates areas of American life far beyond the economic sphere.[4] Robert Wuthnow's very important study of post-World War II religious life, *The Restructuring of American Religion* (1988),184 illustrates the market model's emerging dominance in the area of religion. Wuthnow contends that Americans are as religious in the 1990s as they were forty years ago. He argues that the forms of American piety have changed, not their depth. Immediately following World War II, Americans expressed their piety in the traditional form of church membership and participation. But over the last decades denominational loyalty among American Protestants has weakened. Recent years also have witnessed a shift away from church affiliation to association with a religious special purpose group. This shift betokens an important change in the form of American piety.[5]

The shift away from church affiliation has taken the form of looser ties to the congregation and the denomination to which the local congregation is connected. A culture such as ours, shaped as it is by the therapeutic, the entertaining, and the consumerist morality, will of necessity reinforce the assumptions of religious Americans in this new setting. They are perfectly free to choose the form of their piety and the services [i.e., "ministries"] this form provides. Their choice of form must be "right for them," and this choice will often be made on the basis of the values of "good feeling" and entertainment. Moreover, such assumptions come to shape our very way of construing problems. For example, church-school teachers now attend workshops on topics like "Making the Bible Come Alive." But this way of posing the topic suggests that the problems or shortcomings in our classrooms could not possibly be our fault. The blame for boring church-school sessions must be laid elsewhere. The Bible now appears as the only other candidate to blame for the supposed shortcomings of the church school. We falsely conclude that the Bible is boring and, correlatively, the teacher's task must be to make it "come alive." In other words, the teacher or minister now carries the burden of seeing to it that parishioners are happy and entertained. If the day ever dawns when parishioners feel unhappy or unfulfilled, i.e., bored, they will search elsewhere for a church with the "ministries" which will "meet their needs." In religion as in other facets of American life we live in a buyer's market, and also as in commercial life, the small congregation finds it difficult to offer the religious programs offered by mega-churches. They find the competition for people as difficult as the neighborhood hardware store finds it difficult to attract customers who increasingly patronize Wal-Mart. The same set of dynamics underlies both problems.

Some of us, however, are bothered by the portrait of consumer religion that I have drawn thus far. It disturbs us because it is as such variance with our conception of the church as the people of God, a people who, among other things, embody the normative claims of this God upon their lives. American culture makes it very difficult to practice the life of a disciplined body that seeks to form its members after the measure of the stature of the fullness of

Christ. In fact, our culture exerts daily pressures on us to conform to its consumerist morality. By that I mean that our culture powerfully works on us to become ministers and parishioners who think of the church as an entity that provides people with the programs they want, whose worship is entertaining, and whose criteria of success includes fulfillment and good feelings somewhere very near the top of the list. Furthermore, the pastoral staffs of such churches will feel obligated to incorporate into their ministries those techniques or skills, i.e., expertise, that will enable them to bring about these criteria.

The spectacle of the American church serving under the domination of the consumerist culture presents us with a bleak picture. But the good news is that we are alone in this morass. Ours is not the first age in which the people of God have felt the pressure to live according to the spirit of the age. In premonarchial Israel a set of circumstances somewhat reminiscent of ours led the elders of Israel to the conclusion that their problems would be solved and they would enjoy success if they adopted the methods and expertise of the culture that surrounded them. In the hope of gaining further insight into our situation and some guidance for living through it as the people of God, I turn now to I Samuel, chapters 7, 8, and 12.

2. The Desire for Stability and Destabilizing Hope

First Samuel 7 pictures Israel at a moment in its life when its familiar customs and ways of ordering its affairs had lost the confidence of the community's elders. In the face of Canaanite culture, the persistent threat of the Philistines, and their own growing prosperity, the elders of Israel rapidly lost confidence in the old covenantal religion of Yahweh. Israel's temptation to look for other means by which to secure its existence already manifests itself in chapter 7; in chapter 8 this temptation reaches crisis proportions. In 7:3ff Samuel, the last of Israel's judges, urges the people to, as Brueggmann says,

> Return to Yahweh with all its heart. . . . Israel is to
> have a single heart, a single loyalty devoted only to
> Yahweh. . . . This central affirmation is the core claim of

the Mosaic covenantal faith. This summons requires that Israel look only to Yahweh in every need and every circumstance. In Samuel's time, . . . Israel began to notice other loyalties that looked more promising. Israel began to mix its faith and its loyalty with other loyalties and alternatives seemingly more attractive, more compelling, and more productive (Brueggmann 1990: 49).

Walter Brueggemann describes Israel's situation as one in which the modes of power offered by Samuel seem to the elders to be out of touch with the dominant modes of social order. Samuel called Israel to its covenantal relationship in which Yahweh promised to "save" in response to the "cry" of the people.

In the pattern of cry-answer we are at the core of biblical faith, at one of Israel's most elemental word-patterns and one of its most characteristic acts of faithfulness. To cry to Yahweh is to acknowledge trust in and release in Yahweh . . . [This cry acknowledges] that help must be given because the human person of the human community lacks the resources to secure life . . . [This cry] is . . . therefore, an act of rightly relating to God (50-51).

Despite the ancient covenantal overtones of the cry-answer relation, Israel's elders no longer trusted it to order social power and arrangements. It is as if they said to Samuel, "All this crying to Yahweh and trusting him to answer is okay for the tabernacle, but we live in a real world. We must secure our social and political lives according to the rules by which the real world plays the game." "It is precisely because Samuel's modes of power and faith seemed so unrelated to reality that Israel wanted a king" (55).

We must be prepared to acknowledge the legitimacy of the elders' concern and lack of trust in the old ways. Chapter 8 opens with a scene reminiscent of the days of Eli, only here the sons of Samuel now are those who pervert justice and abuse their position to line their own pockets. Small wonder that the elders of Israel wonder about the public good and decent government when they live in a community where the leadership undermines those necessities of political life (61). The elders were among that segment of Israelite society that had prospered in the settlement of Canaan. They had social and economic concerns that in turn gave them a vested interest in a secure social order. The monarchies of Israel's neighbors offered the elders numerous examples of a way of ordering social and political power alternative to Samuel's covenantalism. The attraction of this alternative technique of social control overcame Israel's attachment to its traditions, and the elders did the unthinkable—they asked for a king, "like the nations."

> The request suggests an intense dispute concerning the character and identity of the community. From its inception at Sinai, it was understood that Israel was chosen by Yahweh and that this chosen community of covenant was not to be like the nations. Rather, Israel was to live its life in the odd and demanding ways of torah and to rely on the inexplicable love and the remarkable promises of Yahweh (Exod. 19:4-6; Deut. 7:7-11). In this dramatic confrontation the elders propose to abandon that self-understanding, that vocation that prized a peculiar form of social organization. Samuel recognizes the implications of the request by the elders. Their request is nothing less than a change in Israel's foundational commitments (v. 6; cf., Jer. 2:11) (62).

Brueggemann comments that Israel's vocation to life in covenant with Yahweh thrust upon the people a peculiar form of social and political power. According to the terms of the covenant, Yahweh pledged to be Israel's God in return for their worship and allegiance. When they cried to Yahweh for help, the covenant assured Israel that Yahweh would hear and answer. The legislation in the Book of Leviticus must be understood as a further explication of Israel's obligations under a covenant that had obvious social and political dimensions. Of course, social and political life under such terms had the effect of distinguishing Israel from its neighbors. The nations were governed by kings, while Israel was governed by Yahweh, whose desires for the people were mediated through judges like Samuel.

In this light, says Brueggmann, the elders'

> Request for a king must be seen as the result of a concern greater than the desire for military protection from the Philistine threat. Kingship . . . is part of a large comprehensive change in social relationships, affecting every dimension of Israelite life. As tribal society with its discrete, independent units experienced political and economic fusion, new patterns of power, wealth, and land control emerged. In this view, monarchy is the culmination of a drive toward centralization, monopoly, kingship, and absolutism, accompanied by the emergence of an enormous economic surplus" (58).

This peculiar relation [of covenant] with Yahweh and the form of social power derived from the relation proved to be a costly embarrassment to Israel. In its restlessness, Israel begins to seek ways to be less peculiar and more "like the nations" (66).

For those of us who think of the church as Israel's successor, the new people of God, the implications of Walter Brueggemann's analysis of 1 Samuel 7 and 8 raise some perplexing and perhaps disturbing questions. Like Israel we are tempted to employ the socio-political arrangements and techniques of the nations. In our case, however, the nations are not Moab and Philistia but the consumerist culture and various schools of thought about management technique. Israel was tempted to employ the techniques of monarchy, learned from the nations. The American church is tempted to employ the skills and techniques of management and organizational expertise in the pursuit of the feelings of well-being. And yet, the church cannot succumb to those temptations without courting a disaster equal to that which befell Israel in the aftermath of her decision to follow after the nations.

Stanley Hauerwas contends that, like Israel, the church is distinguished from other social groups by its polity, which is to say, the politics of remembering.[6] The act of remembering, however, has a particularly destabilizing function among the people of God. For the act of remembering has the particular purpose in Israel of leading to hope. The people of God remember Yahweh's mighty acts of redemption in order that the pain of the present situation might be redeemed in hope of what Yahweh will again do. "In its worship Israel, through remembering, . . . engaged in processing its shared experience through its normative symbols and narratives. As the community does this work [of worship], it finds mediated to it energy, power, authority, assurance, and mandate that are available nowhere else" (Brueggemann 1988: 30). However, as we remember in worship the mighty acts of God, we participate in the making of a new world quite at variance with the presumed world of this present age. "Praise is not a response to a world already fixed and settled, but it is a responsive and obedient participation in a world yet to be decreed and in process of being decreed through this liturgical act" (11). In the hope-filled praise of the people of God, therefore, to remember is to destabilize the present world in favor of the social reality ruled by Yahweh.

Because memory and hope destabilize the social and political arrangements of the presumed world, they will be opposed by entrenched systems of power that have vested interests in the preservation of the present world. The enemies of hope-filled memory are repression, fulfillment, and technique (Brueggemann 88-89). These three conspire to cause the people of God to forget and give up their claim to hope. Fulfillment is particularly interested in stability, for it encourages the people of God to protect what they already possess. "When the present is coterminous with our best dreams, then there is no further dream, no vision toward which to live, and finally no hope" (88-89). But for our considerations here, the most alarming of hope's enemies must be technique. Like Israelite elders, the church's leadership will be tempted to solve its problems and build flourishing communities through recourse to the techniques and expertise of the "nations" that surround it. But the employment of such methods compromises the church no less than the Israelites' request for a king compromised their self-understanding as the people of Yahweh. Of course church ministry and leadership must be competent. "But in the Bible, technique, the capacity to reduce life's mysteries to manageable, discrete elements is embodied in the wise men of Pharaoh, . . . the court magicians of the Joseph story, . . . [and] Nebuchadnezzar who fail. . . . Where do these technocrats live, how do they discern, and for whom? They tend to live in the patronage of the established order. Technique is never democratically distributed, nor is its use neutral. It is always funded and sponsored by the "big house," and so, predictably, is likely to serve those ends" (88-89).

Given the sponsors of technique and expertise, such methods cannot be regarded as neutral. They will serve the established order, the "real world" which we falsely learn to accept as given. As such, these techniques must be seen as the enemies of hope and the new world that hope dares to envision, the world that the people of God dare to believe dawns again whenever they gather to worship God. To dare such belief is to destabilize the present and commits the church to a decidedly counter-cultural stance. To dare such belief is to live hopefully within history without acquiescing to the spirit of the age.

The spirit of our age tells us that people have a right to feel good, to have their needs met. At first glance, the ministry of the church seems tailored to just such an age. Surely the church must care for the same blind, lame, and prisoners to whom Jesus first announced the promise of the dawning reign of God. But Christians who are committed to this end must take care lest their good intentions lead them to a mistaken notion of the church. The church must address the human needs of people, but it must not fall prey to the idea that any need may be legitimately addressed by the church. Moreover, part of the church's ministry is to help people understand the nature of their deepest and truest needs. Most emphatically, it is not the church's role to cater to those who have confused their "needs" with their desires, one of the consumer culture's most common fallacies.

At his trial before Pilate, Jesus said that his kingdom was not of this world. The reign of God is unlike anything in the world. As the sign and witness of that reign, the church is called to be a polity, a social reality, the practices of which are as much unlike the world as God's reign itself differs from conventional worldly wisdom and politics. The church which mistakenly takes up the tools and techniques of the consumerist culture will inevitably fail of that larger calling. Although many of the practices of that culture may seem effective, not all conform to the nature of the church. The church must see to it that its practices conform to its calling. A Roman who lived his life through a set of social practices shaped by his presumed world, Pilate's "reality" prevented him from seeing the reign of God that Jesus incarnated. The American church of the late twentieth century must take care that its assumptions about the real world do not distort our vision of the Lord to whom we are called to witness and whose kingdom and practices still are not of this world.

Chapter Six Notes

1. Lear 1983: 4. Fox and Lears argue that a consumer culture is much larger than our society's ability to mass-produce, mass-market and consume goods and services. In the consumer culture of our time, social elites rule through a pervasive idiom that promises us personal fulfillment. This therapeutic and corporate idiom stands in stark contrast to the individual and moralistic idiom that governed American society in the nineteenth century. Rather than speaking an idiom that promised well-being and happiness, nineteenth century social elites led their society through sponsoring ethical precepts, e.g., McGuffey's Eclectic Reader, which people were encouraged to internalize. Cf. xii.

2. Roger Betsworth, *Social Ethics*, 1990: 83-84. Following Clifford Geertz, Betsworth defines a cultural narrative as "one of the primary ways in which a culture patterns our lives. Through narrative, cultural communities communicate, perpetuate, and develop knowledge about and attitudes toward life. Accordingly, the narratives of a culture are not disinterested observations of experience. They organize experience into a quite definite frame of meaning and seek to teach us to think in the same way" (15). Betsworth's description of American culture's narrative of well-being follows a line of thought developed in several earlier works: *Habits of the Heart*, Bellah, 1985: 13-17 and 113-141; Christopher Lasch, *The Culture of Narcissism*, 1979; and Philip Rieff, *The Triumph of the Therapeutic*, 1968.

3. Anyone who is the parent of a teen-ager has surely heard those words of ultimate condemnation, "This is boring." Lately I have taken to asking my students and my own sons to consider the possibility that boredom is more their problem than another person or thing outside them. I ask them to consider the question, "Why is our boredom usually believed to be the fault of some other person or thing? Where is it written, and on what grounds, that those engaged in public discourse—teachers, ministers, and others, even politicians—are obligated to prevent boredom in their audiences? Those engaged in public discourse have accepted this misplaced responsibility because the age of entertainment has trained them to do so.

4. A particularly pertinent discussion of the extension of the market metaphor and its rationalization of a wide variety of non-economic choices, along with a critique of this extension, can be found in Alan Wolfe, *Whose Keeper? Social Science and Moral Obligation*, 1989, 27-104.

5. More than 800 religious special purpose groups existed at the time Wuthnow published his study. About 300 of these were founded after 1960. Since WW II approximately 500 new religious special purpose groups have been founded. ibid.,pp. 108, 112.

6. Cf. *A Community of Character*, 1981: 9-71, esp. 53-71, "The Moral Authority of Scripture: The Politics and Ethics of Remembering."

The Bible, The Church, and Christian Education

In his fine discussion of Christian morality as friendship with God, Gregory Jones contends that one part of the moral development of Christian disciples entails their participation in several practices (1990: 136ff). Practices are group-sanctioned activities which, in the case of the church, shape our discipleship in reference to our friendship with God. They also place us in the presence of other Christians who are to be counted as our friends. Jones identifies four such practices: baptism, the Lord's Supper, forgiveness-reconciliation, and the interpretation of Scripture. These practices, and perhaps others, are critical to the edification of the church, because they "provide the occasions for forming and transforming people in moral judgment" (136ff). Another way of putting this is to say that as Christians are schooled in these practices their characters are formed—perhaps transformed—into lives that begin to resemble the character of a follower of Jesus.

If Jones' assessment is at all accurate, then we must think about the profoundly moral quality of the church's educational ministry. I am not thinking here about the ethics of teaching or the moral conduct of the learning arena, important topics though they surely are. Rather, I want to quote the Great Commission and say that the mission of the church is to make disciples. But disciples are made, so says Matthew 28:19, through baptism and teaching all that Jesus commanded his followers. Thus the Great Commission presses the church toward its educational ministry, and that project must entail the practices Jones lists. It seems, then, that those who work in any aspect of the church's educational ministry are faced with a task undeniably moral in its implications. This ministry resembles a rope that weaves together several strands: (1) instruction in the Scripture and the arts of biblical interpretation, which necessarily entails (2) life in the story-formed community called the church, which schools us in a particular way of construing the world, which construal then (3) illuminates the moral formation of Christian disciples. To overlook or eliminate any of these three seriously weakens the rope.

The essay that follows should not be read as a blueprint for a congregational program in Christian education. Rather, I propose to examine aspects of each of the three strands in the church's educational ministry. In so doing, I wish to stimulate the thought of those who are involved in this vital dimension of congregational life. Such stimulus will, I hope, lead to ideas that will enrich the body of Christ and enhance the moral formation of those who would follow Jesus.

1. The Bible and Its Interpretation

1.1 What is the Bible?

Some may find the simplicity of this question insulting. Nevertheless, I wish to begin with a common footing, and so I offer a description of the Bible by Walter Brueggemann, one of the finest biblical scholars working today: "The Bible is a shared memory of events that were important to our fathers" (1968: 2). He amplifies this idea by saying that: (1) the Bible records events of the past that previous generations believed important to pass along to subsequent generations; (2) the people of God shared this memory and they share it still, i.e., just as the Bible is not the product of one person's work, so its interpretation must be a communal project; (3) the Bible is not just anyone's memory, but that of our forefathers and foremothers in the faith, those who would "teach us what is good and true" and who nurture us in a particular way of life;

163

and (4) the Bible is about the most important things in life—"meaning, life and death, with what things we must fear and the persons we may trust, with relationships broken and restored, with the problems of guilt and how we may be forgiven" (3-4).

If we accept Brueggemann's description, then some other ideas follow. He describes the Bible in such a way as to appropriately call it the public treasure of the church; the Bible is the book of the people of God. Moreover, if an anthropomorphism might be permitted, the Bible intends to form the moral shape of the people of God. It is instruction for a people called to walk in the way of the Lord, and that means bearing the peculiar stamp of that God.

The Bible is instruction for a community before it is the private guide of individuals. Those who examine the Hebrew or Greek forms of the pronoun "you" in both the Old and New Testaments will discover that, in the wide majority of instances, those pronouns take a plural form. At the very least, such a discovery suggests that the Bible is addressed not so much to individuals as to the *congregation*, whether of Israel or the church, so that the community might become a people worthy of the God of Abraham, Isaac, Jacob, and Jesus. Parenthetically, this insight should mean the immediate cessation of the badly mistaken phrase, "my Bible"—as in "Well, *my* Bible says . . ." This manner of speaking seems clearly outside the Bible's purpose.

To speak of the Bible as a book addressed to a community is a statement surely at odds with the individualistic assumptions of American life in the late twentieth century. A culture that encourages men and women to think of religion as a matter of private choice trains us to read every "you" in the Bible as directed to us, personally and privately. To do so, however, leads to serious mistakes in the interpretation of biblical texts; the Bible is addressed not to an aggregation of individuals but to the congregation of those who live in faith with God and have pledged themselves to live as the faithful followers of God throughout their lives.

1.2 Communities and Interpretation

If the Bible is a communal book, then its interpretation cannot be a matter of purely private judgment. This idea strikes Protestants as heresy, committed as they are to such notions as the priesthood of the believers and the correlative claim that each person has the right of private judgment in matters of scripture interpretation. Nevertheless, it is increasingly apparent that a hermeneutics faithful to biblical traditions will be corporate. Indeed, this seems to have been the process in which the canon itself was formed.

Stated flatly, this means that there is not, nor has there ever been such a thing as *sola scriptura*. It may have been a great slogan for sixteenth century Protestants, but it simply was not true. This judgment must apply even to those groups that have said that they have "no creed but the Bible." In the middle of the nineteenth century, John Williamson Nevin, a German Reformed theologian teaching at Mercersburg Seminary asked the question that reveals the impossibility of this hermeneutical position. Why is it, Nevin asked, that we have so many Christian groups with such different doctrine if, as they claim, each has no creed but the Bible? Nevin's rhetorical question leads to the conclusion that the interpretation of the Bible is never an individual matter. We always read the Bible through a set of eyeglasses, as it were, and these eyeglasses color the words and ideas which we find in the Scripture. The church tradition and the larger culture of which we are parts provide us with these eyeglasses, whether or not we ask for them.

An early Church of God minister and writer, D. Otis Teasley, understood that so-called "private interpretation" was practically impossible and actually dangerous to both individual believer and the community of faith. Teasley said that Catholics and Protestants both erred in their views of the relation between individual reader and the church. In his view the former insisted that the church should determine the meaning of the Scripture for individuals; the latter took the opposite stance. Teasley thought that both positions erred in the extreme. In one case the church usurps individuals' rights of interpretation and "binds her interpretation upon the consciences of men" (1918: 53). On the other hand, "Protestantism . . . lost sight of the relation that should exist between the body of Christ and the individual members of the church" (53). A more truthful approach to this question would result, said Teasley, in a respectful balance between the community and the individual. "The church is not given the supreme right to interpret the Bible for the individual, nor is the individual given the right regardless of unity and peace to interpret the Bible contrary to the general belief of the true church and force his interpretation upon others."

Teasley's insights anticipate a development in later twentieth century scholarship that insists that reading and interpretation cannot take place apart from the existence of what are sometimes called "interpretive communities." Readers do not come to any text as blank slates, ready to have written upon them "the meaning" of the text. Rather, we learn how to read and interpret texts, and the communities of which we are part provide us with the frameworks or paradigms in which we do our interpretive work.

Of course we belong to several communities that have different and often conflicting sets of values. For example, we are simultaneously citizens of nation-states and members of the church, two communities with very different ends and values. Ideas can often take very different shapes depending upon which of these communities provides us with our dominant interpretive paradigm. Take the idea of "freedom," for instance. Citizens of the United States interpret the idea of freedom as an end in itself; freedom is thus a good in its own right often understood to mean the complete absence, or a bare minimum, of restraint. On the other hand, the traditions of the interpretive community called the church cast freedom in a very different light. The Bible never understands freedom as an end in itself but as a *means* to a greater end. Yahweh frees Israel in the Exodus, not so that former slaves may be free, like the desert wind, to do as they please, but that they might serve Yahweh and become a peculiar people committed to justice and mercy. Freedom in the Bible thus turns out to read very differently than the idea of freedom in American political culture. This brief example illustrates how the meanings of even a common idea like freedom can conflict, and these wide variations suggest the presence of interpretive communities that provide us with determinative frameworks with which we make meaning of texts.

The presence of interpretive communities that so profoundly influence the way we come to texts and the meaning we make of them implies that those who interpret Scripture must have decided which community and paradigm will have the privileged position of providing the master images that guide our interpretation. But master images may lose their sharp focus over time as frameworks from other, alien communities encroach upon them. Thus interpreters must always refine the master image as a matter of self-correction. This surely was among the major functions of prophetism in ancient Israel. Further, as interpreters of Scripture we are faced with the never-ending task of critically re-examining previous interpretations in light of contemporary experience. These mutually supportive tasks of refinement and critical re-examination are among the properties of the Hebrew interpretive technique called *midrash*, and it is a skill necessary to the interpretive and moral life of the people of God.

1.3 The Bible, Interpretation, and Education

On the view that I have been developing here, we may now say that the church is the community that is to provide the master image out of which Christians' interpretation of Scripture will grow. That is not to say that communities other than the church have no skills that can help us in our interpretive task, but we must have a starting point and criteria by which to separate wheat from chaff. The Bible and the church can provide those criteria, but only if we have reached a shared understanding of what the Bible is and what its legitimate purposes might be. In other words, skillful and true biblical interpretation depends in large measure on the interpreters' knowledge of both the text and the framework through which the church has taught them to read it. What, then, might be some of the criteria that guide the church's interpretation of and education in the Bible?

Brueggemann suggests that biblical education occurs in two dimensions. On the one hand, education in the Bible is education in *passion*. "Education in passion . . . is nurture into a distinct community which knows itself to be at odds with [the dominant community and its values and assumptions]" (1985: 173). Those who are educated in passion come to acquire certain virtues characteristic of the people of God. The characters of such men and women display: (1) *the ability to cry*, "to feel pain, to articulate the anguish, to sense the pathos and act on it"; (2) *the ability to care*, to welcome the stranger, as Deuteronomy 10:19 says, Love the sojourner therefore; for you were sojourners in the land of Egypt; (3) *the ability to rage*, "a theological act whereby Israel assaults what is or appears to be Yahweh's fickleness, indifference, or infidelity . . . [the people of God] must not be excessively submissive even at the throne of God, for excessive submissiveness to God is most probably allied with excessive conformity to the social powers of the day"; (4) *the ability to hope*, [for] "God will work an unextrapolated, underived newness. . . . Keeping the future open to God's newness (which hope does) serves inevitably to keep the present open and under review, to preclude absolutizing the present. It is that tradition which causes Torah nurtured people to be so impatient, so problematic, so difficult to administer" (175).

Education in the Bible is education in passion. On the other hand, biblical education possesses a dimension Brueggemann calls "perspective." If education in passion forms us to be a people who can cry, care, rage, and hope, its educational partner "consists in the older generation communicating its deposit of tested perspective to the younger generation, and one hopes, having that younger generation appropriate that perspective with respect and discipline (175). With reference to the Hebrew Bible we might think of the prophets as providing an education in passion and the wisdom writings undertaking our education in perspective.

> At the very center of wisdom instruction is a buoyant, confident affirmation of God who presides over . . . [an] orderly social process that produces well-being. It is the link between pragmatic benefit and theological affirmation that makes wisdom instruction so powerful and so convincing. Such teachers are not merely shrewd operators, but they spend their time trying to discern how God presides over the creation and human life (176).

Like biblical education in passion, education in biblical perspective yields important skills: (1) an appreciation of the coherent interrelation of life in all its many aspects; (2) an acknowledgment of life's transcendent mystery even in the midst of these interrelationships; (3) the capacity to critically unmask its own claims to knowledge; and (4) arrival at a trustful submission and yielding to Yahweh and Yahweh's ways (177-178).

The people of God, which is to say the church, is a community committed to the moral formation of its people. The mission of the church is to make disciples. It turns out that making disciples is largely taking up with education in passion and perspective. Canon and community are thus inextricably interrelated. The canon seeks to form a people in the virtues associated with the dimensions of biblical education—passion and perspective, and the people cannot participate in this education unless they understand that they are a people with a particular story that sets them apart and over against the powers who would pretend to rule this world. To read the Bible intelligently and with insight we must live in the hermeneutical circle that holds both canon and community together. Those who nurture the church in the biblical enterprise of education in both passion and perspective must in turn be nurtured by the church in this moral education. The Bible needs the church to accomplish its purpose of raising up a people worthy of the God whose story we read in its pages. The church needs the Bible in order to be a community that can faithfully teach education in passion and perspective.

2. The Educational Task of Interpreting the Biblical Tradition

A recent column by Tim Rutten in the *Los Angeles Times* described one of the long, fire-lit evenings that he and his wife customarily spend listening to traditional storytellers in the local pub of a remote Irish village. Rutten retold two or three of the stories he had heard, but his main point was to assert the importance of narrative or tradition to the human psyche. For years now literary theorists and critics of one theoretical persuasion have argued that humans impose narrative structures on otherwise random events, while other scholars have insisted that human experience possesses an inherently narrative quality. I am not so arrogant as to propose to settle that debate. Rather, I want to suggest that Christian education, as we have considered it already, is essentially the traditioning of the people of God.

In his *Times* column Rutten quoted a woman of County Galway, who once was asked by an anthropologist whether she believed in fairies. She replied, "I do not, sir, but they're there anyway." Whether they are structures imposed to legitimate power or inherent in human experience, narratives and traditions are there, any-way. Beyond asserting their presence, however, I want to argue that tradition is intrinsic to the form of education that the Bible prac-tices among the people of God. In that sense, becoming a Christian and thus a member of the church is much like jumping aboard a moving train. The train had a destination before we became passen-gers; our task, now that we are on board, is to form our lives according to that predetermined goal. In that sense we are not free to be whatever kind of people we choose. The church's destination is neither open to debate nor subject to a vote. Thus Christian edu-cation, cannot be formed according to the consumer interests of parishioners. Rather than "finding an [educational] need and filling it," to borrow a phrase, the purpose of the church's educational ministry is to teach in such a manner as to aid the Bible in its edu-cational project of forming a people who will be morally capable of living lives faithful to the God of Scripture.

2.1 Tradition and Education

> Education . . . is an obscure process by which a per-son's experience is brought into contact with his place and his history. A college can train a person in four years; it can barely begin his education in that time. A person's education begins before his birth in the making of the disciplines, traditions, and attitudes of mind that he will inherit, and it continues until his death under the slow, expensive and uneasy tutelage of his experience (Berry 1972: 103)

Wendell Berry distinguishes training and education, defining the latter as a process that brings together people's experience with their place and their history. That turns out to be a fair description of the idea of education in the Bible. Each generation of Israelites had to be taught to reckon their experience according to the two great truths of the community—the land that Yahweh had promised Abraham and the narratives or traditions through which Israelites learned how they had come to dwell in the land of promise.

In the Old Testament, the young are included in Israel's "narrative imagination." Education in this mode consists in telling and hearing stories that are deeply rooted in the memory and experience of this people, but which are open-ended and can be imaginatively carried in many different directions depending on need, possibility, and circumstance. Israel asserts to its young that *these are the stories*. There can be no other stories. These must be embraced to be who we are. But Israel, at the same time, is enormously open to what these stories say and mean, and thus allows great *freedom in interpretation* (Brueggemann 1985: 173).

Let us examine a story that demonstrates the community's insistent and yet interpretive education of the next generation, 2 Kings 6:8-23. This story illustrates the "world-making power of the biblical traditions and the manner in which they serve to educate their listeners in resistance to the power that claims to define "reality."

In some important respects, we must caution ourselves against the assumption that an unbridgeable chasm separates us from the world of the Bible. It is true that very different assumptions underlie our view of the world from the Bible's. But in other respects, our world and the Bible's are very similar. For example, in both worlds the powerful attempt to legitimate their control and authority through official narrative interpretations. Power, then and now, confers the ability to construct descriptions of "the way things are" and explanations of how they got to be that way. Although we might think such a use of power to be illegitimate, it nevertheless confers the ability to author traditions. Thus investment house financiers like Michael Milken interpret events for stockholders to frame a story that is not at all the way it would be told by the employees of a company about to be dissolved because of the profits available through a leveraged buy out. Like corporate executives,and political leaders of today, the power of Old Testament kings granted them the ability to interpret events according to their point of view. This point of view usually legitimated the authority of royal power. After all, why would power tell a story that might erode power? Power's tendency to construct legitimating traditions can be located in many of the narratives of the Old Testament.

Almost since the beginning of history, chroniclers and historians have focused their attention on kings and political affairs in the belief that they are the thread that connects events and world affairs. Institutional historians succumb to the same fascination with power and the fallacies that it produces. Thus we read histories of churches that are mostly about the clergy and histories of colleges that so emphasize presidents and deans that one would think neither students nor professors ever set foot on the campus. The Bible resists the notion that all power sits on thrones or in leather- upholstered executive swivel chairs. In 2 Kings 6:8-23 we find an example of how the insistent and yet interpretable stories of royal power refuse to allow such power the absolute freedom to shape Israel's world.

The Deuteronomic historian-theologians who gave us such a sweeping view of the life of Israel were also prone to the assumption that the only story that mattered was the story of kings. This tendency may have been more than the historians' assumption; it may also reflect the source of their patronage and their own social class' sense of the proper socio-political order in Israel. Walter Brueggemann contends, however, that the Deuteronomic history does not recount the story of royal power to the absolute exclusion of other possible readings of events. "Specifically and most extensively in the middle of the Omri-Ahab dynasty, the [historian-] theologians break away from the royal recital to give voice to a very different historical memory, expressed in a very different idiom— the stunning narratives concerning Elijah, Elisha and Micaiah. These narratives are extended accounts of the embarrassing footnote of hurt and amazement which the weighty royal report was unable to censor" (1991: 29-30).

Brueggemann describes the Elisha stories as "narratives of amazement" that subvert the story told by royal power. This subversion occurs as these stories create a world that must be seen as a clear alternative to the world constructed by the legitimizing narratives of court historians. The Elisha narrative "creates a world that could be—even though the kings wanted to insist that such a world is not possible. The narrative playfully probes to see what kind of world might exist were the canon of control, the authority of kingship, and subservience to established power not taken too seriously. In 2 Kings 6:8-23 we watch the construction of. . . [this] alternative world" (31).

The story opens in the midst of a war waged on the northern

kingdom of Israel by the king of Aram. This king announced to his staff a plan to waylay and capture the Israelite king, but the latter was warned by "the man of God" (v. 9). Frustrated by this inability to carry out his attack on the Israelite king, the King of Aram determined to locate and plug his security leak. The king dispatched not "plumbers" but a whole army with orders to take the "man of God" captive.

To this point we are told very little about the "man of God". An air of mystery surrounds him and the way he comes to know the secret affairs of kings. His power ranges wide, even to the words kings whisper to their paramours in the privacy of royal bedrooms. The "man of God" may know of the Aramaean king's love-life, but more important to the king is the "man of God's" apparent access to military secrets. Security leaks in the military subvert the world secured by royal domination. Thus the "man of God" and his mysterious knowledge threatened the Aramaean king's presumed world order and his ability to impose that world on others as "reality."

In verse 12 we learn the man of God's name; he is Elisha. Elisha now becomes the center of the story, first as the object of the Aramaean king's passionate determination to regain control of events. In this great passion the king sends an army to capture one man. This in itself is astounding; royal or governmental power is seen to be insecure and fearful of those who do not fear it.

Even modern governments display royal power's insecurity in the face of those who refuse to grant it legitimacy. Near the end of her public life, Dorothy Day, the founder and inspiration of the *Catholic Worker* movement and a pacifist, was paid an official visit by an FBI agent. Day later expressed her amusement at the scene. There she was, a little old lady and a pacifist at that, being questioned by a strapping physical specimen who nevertheless felt compelled to carry a revolver. She playfully wondered what it was that he so feared in the *Catholic Worker* office that he carried a gun to protect himself. Similarly, the story of Elisha surely means to poke fun at the futility of the Aramaean king; against Yahweh, no army is large enough, no weapon possesses sufficient destructive power.

In verses 15-19 the locus of the story shifts from the Aramaean king to Elisha's house. Brueggemann reads this shift as marginalizing the Aramaean king insofar as he is an actor in the story; from now on he will be the recipient of action rather than the initiator. "And the narrative itself displaces royal power and focuses attention and interest on the real actors in the historical process"—God, Elisha and his servant (32).

The Aramaean army had surrounded Elisha's house during the night. The next morning his servant awakened and set about the morning chores. When he went outside, the servant discovered the trap in which he and his master apparently had been caught. Out of his great fear and anxiety the servant asks the most logical of questions, "Which way are we to turn?" and receives from Elisha an answer that probably offered scarce comfort, "Do not be afraid, for those who are on our side are more than those on theirs."

Elisha responds to his servant's fear with a prayer. Elisha asks God, not that the boy's fear will be removed, but that he will be given the sight with which to see as Elisha. The prophet asks more of Yahweh. Not only does he request sight for his servant, but Elisha also asks Yahweh to blind the Aramaean army. In this prayer, then, Elisha asks for a great reversal in which the blind receive a sight that conforms to a different way of construing the world, and those who see according to worldly power and wisdom lose the sight they have. Yahweh answers Elisha's prayer, and the young man sees. "He sees as he had not seen. He sees that the reality of power in the world is not as the king had taught him to believe. He sees apart from the dominant ideology in which he had been schooled. . . . The prayer of Elisha has reshaped and redefined the world for the boy. The prophet has known, and now the boy knows, what is unknown to the kings" (32).

The story of Elisha and the King of Aram comes to a strange conclusion after this climactic reversal. The blind, pitiful Aramaean army of the impotent king is led to Samaria, the capital of the northern kingdom, and unwittingly placed in the very jaws of death. Elisha prays once again and the army's sight is restored. Terror flashes through the hapless Aramaeans as they realize their desperate situation, while Israel's king asks the prophet for permission to kill them. That the king must secure Elisha's permission surely reveals the story's opinion that we are now on a very different footing. Neither kings nor presidents are accustomed to asking permission of religious people,[1] but the king of Israel is now as much a suppliant as the Aramaean captives. Elisha tells the king that there is to be no blood bath. Instead, the Israelites are ordered to serve the Aramaeans a feast, after which they go home. "And the Aramaean raids on Israel ceased" (v. 23).

2.2 Tradition and World-Making

Earlier I quoted Brueggemann's observation that Israel educated its young through including them in narratives that it *insisted* were their inheritance and yet that they could *interpret*. The story of Elisha and the Aramaean army illustrates this educational mode.

That this is Israel's story is non-negotiable. Surely the kings and politicians of this world would like ordinary and small people to forget such a story. Those who presume to form the narratives by which they would have us live would hide this story from us if they could. Who of us can name any king or president who would like us to know stories that tell how weapons and armies were foiled of their purpose? Regardless of its designs and desires, royal power may not expunge this story from Israel's memory. That is non-negotiable.

Since this story's presence in our memory is non-negotiable, it offers us the opportunity to interpret the all-too-familiar presumed world of the powerful in ways that are more hopeful. This reinterpretation offers us a reading of events as directed toward "power for life," in Brueggemann's words, rather than the "power for death" of the world of dominant assumptions. Like the servant-boy, we do not see, and the story of Elisha and the Aramaean army offers us the possibility of construing a world according to the vision of Elijah.

In personal and public life, to be able to see the working of God that unfaith cannot see is what permits the overpowering conclusion that "we are more than conquerors through him who loved us." "If we are unable to see the horses and chariots of Yahweh that overwhelm the enemy, then in fact we have nothing important to say in the face of death. The alternative to such daring seeing is to be defeated, to abandon the subversive dream, to nullify our baptism, and to settle for a royal reading of reality. That leaves the king and his army finally in charge"(Brueggemann 1991: 37). This text calls us to reexamine how and what we see .

Vision finally is a matter of character; we see the world, we construe it, according to the kind of persons we are. Our characters are shaped by stories and communities. The church's educational ministry is this very important matter of character transformation such that we become people who see the world that God sees. Our lives are shaped as our place and our story are merged with our experience. For people of the Bible, the result of this shaping process called education will be that the dominant assumptions of this world will be undermined by eyes that see the armies of the Lord ranged on the hills about us.

3. The Educational Formation of the Congregation

> [When] a community loses its memory, its members no longer know one another. How can they know one another if they have forgotten or have never learned one another's stories? If they do not know one another's stories, how can they know whether or not to trust one another? People who do not trust one another do not help one another, and moreover they fear one another. And this is our predicament now. Because of a general trust and suspicion, we not only lose one another's help and companionship, but we are all now living in jeopardy of being sued (Berry 1990: 157).

Through the second half of 1991 and almost all of 1992 the United States' news media force fed their readers and listeners a steady diet of news about "the economy". Those who remember this diet will recall how frequently we were told that the economy was sick; we were living through "hard times." Everybody then wanted to know when those hard times would end, and so we looked to economic indicators for some hint of the future. We anxiously awaited statistical information like monthly unemployment figures and factory orders. Ever more arcane sources of information were searched for answers to questions about the duration of the economy's illness. I recall learning that the economy might be improving because manufacturers had begun ordering more cardboard shipping containers. Like oracles in the ancient world, economic forecasters were consulted with great urgency and little real knowledge of the future. I must confess to a suspicion of the closest correlation between economists who pored over all those indicators and the diviners who once sought hints of the future in the kinks of sheep's intestines.

Our contemporary use of the word differs considerably from earlier usages, and it may be that comparing these variant meanings may help us learn something about what it means to be the community called the church and how that community is nurtured. As I have tried to say in the previous sections of this essay, ultimately the Bible and the church's educational ministry share the same purpose—the moral formation of the people of God. I have stressed the importance of thinking of the church as a community, and for that reason a consideration of the notion of "economy" may prove both interesting and useful as a summary.

3.1 Economy as Household

Contemporary use of the word "economy" principally refers to the systems we employ to trade goods and services, which means it has much to do with money. Thus we have come to think that a healthy economy means that many people possess the ability to purchase the goods and services they believe they need or perhaps want. Hard times signify the opposite. Economists would probably quarrel with my definition, but at this point I am more concerned with popular usage than with the technical definitions of specialists. This rather narrow interpretation of "the economy" will lead to surprises for its careless or unreflective users.

In the late 1980s and early 1990s Americans have become accustomed to comparing their economy with those of other nations, especially Japan. President Bush's 1992 Asian trade trip accomplished little except to intensify the belief of many Americans that Japan's trading practices were to blame for hard times in America. If the Japanese would play fair, ran the argument, the health of the American economy would be restored. That this was a rather myopic view of "the economy" was born out by an incident that occurred in Australia during Mr. Bush's stopover there. Australian grain farmers took advantage of this occasion to ask the president to stop federal subsidies of American farm products. These subsidies were having the effect of artificially depressing the price of farm commodities world-wide. In effect, Australian farmers hoisted Bush on his own petard; they merely asked the president to see to it that his government played by the same rules as he intended on asking the Japanese to follow.

This ironic incident points us in the direction of an earlier and more comprehensive definition of this word *economy*. Its origins lay in ancient Greece, whose language gave us the word *oikonomia* which is simply transliterated into this word which is now on everybody's lips. *Oikonomia* derives from the Greek word for "house," *oikia*, and it refers to the wise and careful management of the affairs of the household. In Ephesians 2:19 Paul tells his readers that they are "fellow citizens with God's people, members of God's household" (NEB). Similarly, Paul advises the Galatians to "work for the good of all, especially members of the household of faith" (6:10, NEB). Here household does not mean "family," certainly not in the modern sense of the nuclear family. Instead, we should read household to mean "all who live under the roof." In the ancient world a household would include many who were unrelated to the head of the house. Thus Paul's reference to the church as a house-hold should call to mind another of his holistic metaphors for the church, i.e., the body. A household is in this sense a body politic where people's lives were understood as extensions of a single organic community. Therefore an economy is an integrated system where each element affects, and is affected by, the life and health of the others. This classic definition of economy thus has much in common with another word now current in our vocabulary, "ecology," the notion of the broadest and most intensive possible interrelatedness of things.

3.2 Story-Formed Communities

People in our society and our time have become accustomed to thinking individualistically. We tend strongly to the point of view that we alone are responsible for our actions and choices. As long as we harm no others, there is no reason why we cannot do as we please. Although the erosion of our environment and the growing awareness that ours is a global village should prompt us to think of ourselves according to the classic definition of economy, there is only slight evidence that this is the case. We stubbornly remain attached to this notion that each of us can choose according to our individual tastes and predispositions. The fact that we live in a world economy challenges some of Americans' most cherished assumptions about the freedom of the individual. But these assumptions nevertheless form Americans' "assumed reality," and we are irritated by the suggestion that we may not be able to do as we please as long as our actions do not harm others.

At present, however, we are being pressed within and without American culture to reconsider the relationship between people and the communities of which they are members. One might wish that the church would form a powerful counter-example to this extreme individualism; for the local church is not an *aggregation* of individuals, but a *congregation* of the faithful whose lives are being formed to be a people worthy of the God of the Bible.

Stanley Hauerwas tells an interesting and entertaining theological and moral tale as an exposition of Richard Adams' political novel, *Watership Down* (1981:9-35). This story also argues for a particular conception of the church as a "story-formed community" as its challenges our society's dominant assumptions about the relationship between individuals and their communities.

Watership Down is a fable that tells the story of a warren of rabbits who, when driven from their home, must find a place to rebuild their community. Their search involves a long journey during which they encounter rabbits from several different warrens with forms of political organization highly unusual for rabbits. In every case, the rabbits of Watership Down find it necessary to leave these unusual rabbit communities. Failure to do so would mean the loss of their identity or character as rabbits.

Hauerwas uses this story to score several criticisms against the modern churches which have been so deeply corrupted by the Enlightenment political liberalism of American culture. Unlike American political thought, says Hauerwas, the church cannot be a community founded on a social contract enacted by individuals. The church does not exist on the basis of a decision made by a collection of individuals who take a vote to authorize its organization. Rather, theologically speaking, the church comes into being, and indeed lives, through the prior call of God. Paul speaks of the church as the body of Christ, and Christians are members thereof.

Thus the polity of the church is not an assemblage of prior existing individuals, but the grafting into a prior existing body of those who have discovered that they cannot live apart from it.

The formation of Christian disciples occurs in many different venues within the life of the congregation. Our lives are formed in worship through the activities of prayer and preaching. The ordinances of the church are important sensory experiences of memory and character formation. Richard Bondi describes these and other occasions of Christian moral formation in his fine article "The Elements of Character" (1984: 201-218). He speaks particularly of the need for character formation to include "proclamation, education and evocation" (215). The story of the God who will not abandon the world to its own sin and alienation must be proclaimed. This story must also be told in such a way that it strikes home in the very core of our being. Of course, telling this story within the context of the church's educational ministry also becomes an essential aspect of the formation of Christian disciples. It seems only appropriate that I illustrate this last claim by way of a story.

Some time ago my Sunday school class experienced a most remarkable hour. The lessons written for the adult Sunday school curriculum for February 1992 formed a unit drawing on some of the great prayers of the Bible. Jesus' "High Priestly Prayer" in John 17 provided the basis for the lesson, but in a very real sense, this lesson was anticipated and prepared by the lesson on the Lord's Prayer we had studied the previous week. Our class customarily expresses both its concerns and its joys at the session's beginning. We believe that our prayers are among the most important expressions of our love and care for one another, so we have developed the practice of listening attentively to all who speak during this part of our session. A woman, visiting our class for the very first time, spoke up during these moments. Through tears and halting speech she told us of her desperate need to find a group of people who would not reject her. Although not in detail, she told us of the deep pain in her past, hurts which had so scarred her as to make it hard to believe that God could give her any gift of goodness. I could not imagine the depth of pain that pushed her to overcome the reticence that naturally accompanies most of us when we visit a group for the first time. She told us that she hoped that we would not reject her as others had in the past. Other class members also expressed their own needs and cares, and then we prayed for all.

After prayer we turned to the lesson. When the reading of the scripture text had been completed, I asked the class one of the questions that appeared in the student handbook, "What would you say if presented with your last opportunity to speak to some person or group?" For a while we remembered what we had said to children who were about to leave for college or the military. Then our conversation took a somber, reflective turn. A woman whose elderly father had recently succumbed to leukemia told us that she wanted to recount the last few minutes of his life. She said that she would have told us sooner, but her memory of her father's passing was still raw and painful and she feared that we might grow impatient with her tears. She told us, anyway, of the inspiration and tenderness of the church and her family as they surrounded her father's bed. Then a grandmother told us through her tears the details of the needless death of her infant grandchild. An older man spoke of his fear at the estrangement he felt between him and one of his children and said that he wanted to repair their relationship because so much remained to be said. Then another class member observed that perhaps the most important thing is that we live in such a way that nothing would be left to say if some event or person were to deny us this opportunity.

By the time all of this talking and listening had run its course, our regular closing time had long since passed. I had asked only one of six questions suggested for our discussion in the student handbook. We did not acquire much new information, since most of our class members were doubtless familiar with John 17. Acquiring information is but one of the lessons learned during the Sunday school hour. Sunday school is one of the places in the church's educational ministry where we hear the story of forgiveness and loving acceptance that is the gospel and then have immediate opportunity to embody that story. It is one of the places in the life of the church where we have virtually simultaneous opportunities for hearing the story of God, interpreting that story and acting upon it.

On this Sunday the people in our class witnessed extraordinary expressions of pain from many of the people sitting in the same circle. The class received those stories and the pain they recounted as if that pain was their own. We do not act this way naturally; it is an acquired skill—a virtue. We have been together as a class for about three years, and in that course of time the traditions of Christianity, the stories of God, Israel, Jesus, and the church, have been doing their quiet work on us. We are more patient, more hospitable, less harsh in our judgments, less angry—in a word, more loving than we were before our class began. On this particular Sunday I witnessed the work of the household of faith who refused to allow some to suffer their pain in silent loneliness. That community, formed by the biblical story, took on its members' pain because, like any body, the suffering of some is the suffering of all. Our Sunday school class is being formed by a story that teaches us that our lives do not flourish as individual, heroic mastery over circumstance, but as members of a beloved community that sustains us through tragedy and joy.

Chapter Seven Notes

1. On the eve of the opening of "Operation Desert Storm," President George Bush heard from his own bishop an interpretation of events not to the President's liking, whereupon Mr. Bush found another representative of the clergy who offered an interpretation and a moral approval more to the President's preference.

Bibliography

Gospel Trumpet (G.T.)

1881. D. S. Warner. (June 1): 2.
1885. D. S. Warner. (Dec 1): 1.
1886. Camp Meeting announcement (Apr. 15): n.d.
1893. D. S. Warner. "The Ministers of God See Eye to Eye" (Dec. 28): 4.
1895. Nelson, Thomas and Charles Akers. "News from the Field" (Feb. 7): n.p.
1898. "Salvation Life in Jail" (July 14): 6.
1899. "Should We Go to War?" (Apr. 14): 4.
1903. J. C. Blaney. "The Treasury Box" (July 23): 6.
1904. Byrum, E. E. "Tithing" (Mar. 24): 4.
1915. Berry, R. L. "The Tithing System Compared with the New Testament System." (Sept. 16): 8.
1916. Hopwood, W. "Field Reports: England" (Feb. 24): 14.
1916. Stewart, Faith. "India: The Shelter Cut[t]ack" (May 25): 12.
1919. "The Meetings of the Young People at the Anderson Campmeeting" (July 3): 18-19.
1960. "Does It Make Any Difference?" (Feb. 14): 3.
1960. "From Readers" (Oct 23): 16.

Anderson, J. Grant. 1921. *Sex Life and Home Problems.* Anderson, Ind: Gospel Trumpet Company.
Bellah, Robert N., et. al. 1985. *Habits of the Heart: Individualism and Commitment in American Life.* Berkeley: University of California Press.
Berry, Wendell. 1972. *A Continuous Harmony: Essays Cultural and Agricultural.* New York: Harcourt Brace Jovanovich.
_____. 1990. "God and Country." In *What Are People For?* San Francisco: North Point Press.
_____. 1990. "The Work of Local Culture." In *What Are People For?* San Francisco: North Point Press.
Betsworth, Roger. 1990. *Social Ethics: An Examination of America's Moral Traditions.* Louisville: Westminster/John Knox.
Bondi, Richard. 1984. "The Elements of Character" *Journal of Religious Ethics* 12, no. 2 (Fall): 201- 218.
Brown, C. E. 1931. *A New Approach to Christian Unity.* Anderson, Ind: Gospel Trumpet Company.
_____. 1954. *When Souls Awaken.* Anderson, Ind: Gospel Trumpet Company.
_____. 1951. *When the Trumpet Sounded.* Anderson, Ind: Warner Press.
Brueggemann, Walter. 1968. *Confronting the Bible: A Resource and Discussion Book for Youth.* NY: Herder and Herder.
_____. 1990. *First and Second Samuel: Interpretation, A Bible Commentary for Teaching and Preaching.* Louisville: John Knox Press.
_____. 1987. *Hope within History.* Atlanta: John Knox Press.

_____. 1991. *Interpretation and Obedience: From Reading to Faithful Living.* Minneapolis: Fortress Press.

_____. 1988. *Israel's Praise: Doxology Against Idolatry and Ideology.* Philadelphia: Fortress Press.

_____. 1985. "Passion and Perspective: Two Dimensions of Education in the Bible." *Theology Today* (July).

Callen, Berry, compiler. 1985. *The Assembly Speaks.* Anderson, Ind: Warner Press.

"The Church and Its Responsibility to the Community." 1949. *Senior Youth* 83-88. (Sept. 11). Anderson, Ind: Warner Press.

Dieter, Mel. 1980. *The Holiness Revival of the Nineteenth Century.* Metuchen, N. J: Scarecrow Press.

Fox, JoAnn, compiler. 1987. *Press On, I'll Meet You at the Gate: Memoirs of Daisy Virginia Maiden Boone.* Capitola, Calif: Van Winkle Press.

Fox, Richard Wightman and T. J. Jackson Lears, eds. 1983. *The Culture of Consumption.* New York: Pantheon Books.

Hatch, Nathan. 1989. *The Democratization of American Christianity.* New Haven: Yale University Press.

_____. 1970. *The Protestant Experience in America.* NY: Dial Press.

Hauerwas, Stanley. 1988. "The church as God's New Language." *In Christian Existence Today: Essays on Church, World and Living In Between.* Durham, N.C: Labyrinth Press.

_____. 1981. *A Community of Character: Toward a Constructive Christian Social Ethic.* Notre Dame: University of Notre Dame Press.

_____. 1990. "Companions on the Way: The Necessity of Friendship." *Asbury Theological Journal* 45, no. 1 (Spring).

_____. 1981. "A Story-Formed Community: Reflections on Watership Down." In *A Community of Character: Toward a Constructive Christian Social Ethic.* Notre Dame: University of Notre Dame Press.

Hauerwas, Stanley and William Willimon. 1989. *Resident Aliens: Life in the Christian Colony.* Nashville: Abingdon Press.

Jones, Charles E. 1974. *Perfectionist Persuasion: The Holiness Movement and American Methodism, 1867-1936.* Metuchen, N.J: ScarecrowPress.

Jones, L. Gregory. 1990. *Transformed Judgment: Toward a Trinitarian Account of the Moral Life.* Notre Dame: University of Notre Dame Press.

Jordan, Wilfred and Richard Willowby, eds. 1991. *The National Association of the Church of God: Diamond Jubilee.* Anderson, Ind: Warner Press.

Kern, Richard. 1974. *John Winebrenner: Nineteenth Century Reformer.* Harrisburg, Pa: Central Publishing House.

Lasch, Christopher. 1979. *The Culture of Narcissism.* NY: W.W. Norton.

Lash, Nicholas. 1986. "Performing the Scriptures." In *Theology on the Way to Emmaus* 37-46. London: SCM Press.

Lears, T. J. Jackson and Richard Wightman Fox. 1983. "From Salvation to Self-Realization: Advertising and the Therapeutic Roots of the Consumer Culture, 1880-1930." In Richard Wightman Fox and T. J. Jackson Lears, eds., *The Culture of Consumption* 3-38. New York: Pantheon Books.

Lightfoot, J. B., ed and trans. 1956. "The Epistle to Diognetus." In *The Apostalic Fathers*. Reprint Edition. Grand Rapids, Mich: Baker Book House.

Marsden, George. 1984. "Introduction." In *Evangelicalism and Modern America* vii-xix. Grand Rapids: Eerdman's Publishing Company.

Marty, Martin. 1970. *Righteous Empire: The Protestant Experience in America*. New York: Dial Press.

McClendon, James. 1986. *Systematic Theology*. Vol. 1. *Ethics*. Nashville: Abingdon Press.

Miller, Perry. 1961. *The New England Mind: From Colony to Province*. Cambridge: Harvard University Press.

Morrison, John A. 1962. *As the River Flows*. Anderson, Ind: Anderson College Press.

National Association of the Church of God Historical Report, 1917-1974. n.d. West Middlesex, Pa: n.p.

Naylor, C. W. 1925. *God's Will and How to Know It*. Anderson, Ind: Gospel Trumpet Company.

Neal, Hazel G. and Axchie A. Bolitho. 1982. *Madam President: The Story of Nora Hunter*. Revised by Marie Meyer. Anderson, Ind: Warner Press.

Nelson, Thomas. 1907. *Home, Health and Success*. Anderson, Ind: Gospel Trumpet Company.

Neuhaus, Richard John. 1987. *The Catholic Moment: The Paradox of the Church in the Postmodern World*. NY: Harper and Row.

Peters, John Leland. 1954. *Christian Perfection and American Methodism*. Nashville: Abingdon Press.

Phelps, J. W. 1917. "Introduction." In *Yearbook of the Church of God* 3. n.p.

Postman, Neil. 1985. *Amusing Ourselves to Death: Public Discourse in the Age of Show Business*. NY: Penguin Books.

Reardon, Robert A. 1979. *The Early Morning Light*. Anderson: Warner Press.

Rieff, Philip. 1968. *The Triumph of the Therapeutic*. NY: Harper and Row.

Riggle, H.M. 1918. *Christ's Kingdom and Reign*. (Anderson, Ind: Gospel Trumpet.

_____. 1919. *Christ's Second Coming and What Will Follow*. Anderson, Ind: Gospel Trumpet Company.

_____. 1943. *Jesus Is Coming Again*. Anderson, Ind: Gospel Trumpet Company.

_____. 1899. *The Kingdom of God and the One Thousand Years' Reign*. Moundsville, W. Va: Gospel Trumpet Publishing Company.

Riggle, H. M. and D. S. Warner. 1903. *The Cleansing of the Sanctuary*. Moundsville: Gospel Trumpet Company.

Roberts, Florence. 1911. "A Visit to a Rescue Home." *Missionary Herald* II, no. 12 (Dec.).

_____. 1912. "How a Fashionable Church Loved the Lost." *Missionary Herald* III, no. 1 (Jan).

Rutter, Jenny C. 1899. *Mothers' Counsel to Their Sons*. Anderson, Ind: Gospel Trumpet Company.

_____. 1899. *Letters of Love and Counsel for 'Our Girls.'* Anderson, Ind: Gospel Trumpet Company.

Schell, William G. 1911. "Biblical Trace of the Church." In *Select Hymns* Anderson, Ind: Gospel Trumpet Company.

Smith, F. G. 1908. *The Revelation Explained*. Anderson, Ind: Gospel Trumpet Company.

Smith, John W. V. 1955. *Heralds of a Brighter Day*. Anderson, Ind: Gospel Trumpet Company.

_____. *The Quest for Holiness and Unity*. Anderson, Ind: Warner Press, 1980.

Smith, Uriah. 1882. *Thoughts, Critical and Practical, on the Book of Daniel and the Revelation*. Battle Creek, Mich: Review and Herald Publishing Association.

Stoeffler, Ernest F. 1971. *The Rise of Evangelical Pietism*. Leiden: E. J. Brill Publishers.

Sykes, Stephen. 1984. *The Identity of Christianity*. Philadelphia: Fortress Press.

Tasker, George P. 1924. *An Appeal to the Free and Autonomous Churches of Christ in the Fellowship of the Evening Light*. Calcutta, India: privately published.

_____. 1981. Qtd. in Lester A. Crose, *Passport for a Reformation*. Anderson, Ind: Warner Press.

Teasley, D. O. 1918. *The Bible and How to Interpret It*. Anderson, Ind: Gospel Trumpet Company.

"They Speak for God?" 1969. *Youth II*. (Oct. 12). Anderson, Ind: Warner Press.

Warner, D. S. 1880. *Bible Proofs of a Second Work of Grace*. Goshen, Ind: E.U. Mennonite Publishing Society.

_____. n.d. *The Church of God: What the Church Is and What It is Not*. n.p.

_____. n.d. *Salvation, Present, Perfect, Now or Never*. Moundsville, W. Va: Gospel Trumpet Company.

_____. 1989. "The Bond of Perfectness." In *Worship the Lord: Hymnal of the Church of God*, no. 330.

Warner, D. S. and H. M. Riggle. 1903. *The Cleansing of the Sanctuary*. Moundsville, W. Va: Gospel Trumpet Company.

Wickersham, H. C. 1894. *Holiness Bible Subjects*. Grand Junction, Mich: Gospel Trumpet Company.

Winebrenner, John. 1868. *Doctrine and Practical Sermons*. Lebanon, Pa: Published by the Authority of the General Eldership of the Church of God.

Wolfe, Alan. 1989. *Whose Keeper? Social Science and Moral Obligation*. Berkeley: University of California Press.

Worker's Bulletin. 1911. Anderson, Ind: Gospel Trumpet Company (Jan.): n.p.

Wuthnow, Robert. 1988. *The Restructuring of American Religion*. Princeton: Princeton University Press .